WIDER PEACEKEEPING

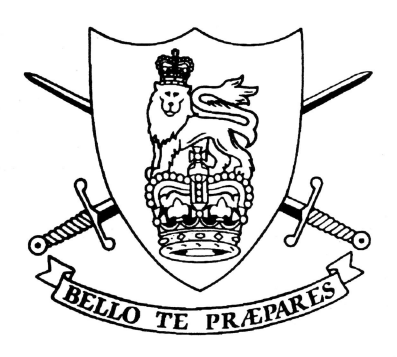

BELLO TE PRÆPARES

London: HMSO

ISBN 0 11 772685 0

This report has also been produced as:

The Army Field Manual Volume 5, Operations other than war, Part 2.

Prepared under the direction of the Inspector General Doctrine and Training on behalf of the Chief of the General Staff.

Please note:
This book was written as one of a series of Army Field Manuals.
Readers will therefore see referencs to AFM(s) and 'the manual'.

ARMY FIELD MANUAL

WIDER PEACEKEEPING

CONTENTS

CHAPTER THREE - OPERATIONAL TASKS

CHAPTER FIVE - OPERATIONAL TECHNIQUES

CHAPTER SIX - PLANNING FOR OPERATIONS

FOREWORD

1. **Introduction**. The term 'Wider Peacekeeping' describes the wider aspects of peacekeeping that, for the British Army, have become more prominent post Cold War.

2. **Aim**. The aim of AFM Wider Peacekeeping is to provide guidance to field commanders and their staffs in the conduct of Wider Peacekeeping operations.

3. **Terminology**. Wider Peacekeeping operations represent a dynamic area of doctrinal development and there is as yet no unanimous international agreement on the definitions of terms or categories of activity. Whilst attempting to employ terms that are generally acceptable to most diplomatic, regional and military communities, this manual seeks to avoid undue dependence on definitions and categories but concentrates instead on conveying ideas that should survive further developments in terminology.

4. **Past Experience**. The term 'Wider Peacekeeping' is original and the scope of its associated operations broad. Notwithstanding the relatively fresh context of such activities, the kinds of operation covered are not new to the British Army. In the latter half of this century our Army amassed a wealth of unique experience in counter insurgency, counter terrorist and peacekeeping operations, maintaining a remarkably successful record. Although the first two are, of course, very different from the latter, many of the doctrinal principles and techniques formulated as a result of this experience apply to Wider Peacekeeping operations and this manual draws extensively on such experience in the hope that it may be useful to others.

5. **Scope**. This manual describes the nature of Wider Peacekeeping, setting the subject in its historical and doctrinal context, and covering the environment, conceptual approach, tasks, principles, techniques and planning requirements pertaining to such operations as well as the training and education which they demand. It explains where Wider Peacekeeping sits in Peace Support Operations as a whole but it is not concerned with the conduct of Peace Enforcement (to be covered in another AFM). It explains how to conduct Wider Peacekeeping and, crucially, how to avoid being drawn into Peace Enforcement unwittingly or unwillingly.

6. **Approach**. As a tactical level manual, 'Wider Peacekeeping' seeks to address the needs of field commanders and their staffs at levels ranging from formation to sub-unit and below. Given this span, as well as the broad range of scenarios and tasks required in Wider Peacekeeping operations, the manual does not set out to tell the reader *what* to think. Nor does it furnish him with detailed instructions for every situation. Rather it suggests *how* to think about Wider Peacekeeping, advancing general guidelines which might be applied to a variety of situations. In this way the manual seeks to shape the tactical commander's intellectual process in *approaching* Wider Peacekeeping operations. It therefore exposes its underlying conceptual approach and sets a broad perspective on the issues described, concentrating on reasoned principles in preference to prescriptive applications.

7. ***Application***. Every Wider Peacekeeping situation will be different. This manual therefore seeks to enable field commanders and their staffs to apply creatively the approaches and principles described in order to address the particular circumstances they face. The manual may prove useful to both military and non-military agencies of the international community and is intended as a framework for further doctrinal discussion and development with the United Nations, allies, regional organizations, academic institutions and other bodies.

8. ***Interim Issue***. This manual is being issued as an interim edition because of the dynamic nature of doctrinal development in this area and because this manual will subsequently be amalgamated with AFM Vol V Part 1 "Peacekeeping Operations" which was produced in 1988. It is intended that the whole area of Peace Support Operations will be covered in an ADP supported by AFMs for peackeeeping and peace enforcement.

September 1994   Director General Land Warfare

CHAPTER ONE

INTRODUCTION

"Tis not hard, I think,
For men so old as we to keep the peace."

William Shakespeare

SECTION ONE - BIRTH OF THE UNITED NATIONS

1. The League of Nations was created in the aftermath of the First World War. In the words of the preamble to its Covenant the League's purpose was to: "promote international cooperation and to achieve international peace and security". It proved singularly unsuccessful. The League alienated the international powers defeated in the First World War and failed to hold together even the victorious allies - indeed the United States never became a member. In the 1920s and 30s the former allies of the First World War drifted apart and disarmed whilst international powers outside the League took to dictatorship and rearmament. One of the League's last acts was to expel the Soviet Union for its attack on Finland in 1939. The

> CONTENTS
>
> BIRTH OF THE UNITED NATIONS
>
> UN CHARTER AND PEACEKEEPING
>
> SCOPE OF MANUAL
>
> ORGANIZATION OF THE UN
>
> OPERATION OF THE UN
>
> PEACEKEEPING DURING THE COLD WAR
>
> A CHANGED SECURITY ENVIRONMENT
>
> WIDER PEACEKEEPING
>
> DEFINING SUCCESS

League of Nations was powerless to prevent the world's descent into a second global war.

2. The United Nations was created in 1945. Like the League of Nations, it was based on the principle of the victorious wartime powers ruling the peace. Unlike the former League, however, the UN made considerable efforts to reconcile and assimilate those peoples defeated in the previous war. The rapid growth of its membership because of decolonization also gave new nations a voice and influence that they had never had before.

SECTION TWO - THE UN CHARTER AND PEACEKEEPING

3. *United Nations Charter*. The UN Charter was drafted at the San Francisco Conference in 1945. Its first article states that a main purpose of the UN is "to maintain international peace and security". The Charter provides the terms of reference for the various elements of the UN in fulfilling this responsibility. Chapter VI of the UN Charter provides for the pacific settlement of disputes by a variety of peaceful measures including negotiation, enquiry, mediation, conciliation, arbitra-

tion and judicial settlement (Article 33). Chapter VII, on the other hand, is essentially coercive and designed to deal with threats to peace, breaches of the peace and acts of aggression perpetrated by sovereign states. Through Chapter VII the UN Security Council is empowered to investigate alleged violations and then determine measures to be taken against the states concerned. These measures can include political and economic pressure (Article 41) and the use of force (Article 42). Coalition operations in Korea, against Iraq and in Somalia were enforcement actions authorized by the UN Security Council. The full text of the UN Charter is set out at Annex A.

4. **Peacekeeping**. Peacekeeping is not specifically provided for in the Charter of the UN which makes no mention of the word. Peacekeeping, which requires the cooperation of the parties to the conflict in question, has evolved as a pragmatic response to a variety of international conflicts which have been placed on the UN agenda over the years. In effect, peacekeeping sought to settle disputes through the medium of pacific third party initiatives. Notwithstanding its limitations, peacekeeping has often proved a valuable technique for the control and resolution of conflicts.

SECTION THREE - THE SCOPE OF THIS MANUAL

5. **Peace Support Operations**. Peace Support Operations is the generic term used to describe those military operations in which UN-sponsored multinational forces may be used. To set their relative context, the three categories of Peace Support Operations are described as follows:

    a. *Peacekeeping*. Operations carried out with the consent of the belligerent parties in support of efforts to achieve or maintain peace in order to promote security and sustain life in areas of potential or actual conflict.

    b. *Wider Peacekeeping*. The wider aspects of peacekeeping operations carried out with the general consent of the belligerent parties but in an environment that may be highly volatile.

    c. *Peace Enforcement*. Operations carried out to restore peace between belligerent parties who do not all consent to intervention and who may be engaged in combat activities.

6. **Military Activities**. The types of military activity which will usually be undertaken within each of the above are categorized as follows:

PEACEKEEPING

> Observer Missions
> Interposition

WIDER PEACEKEEPING

    Conflict Prevention
    Demobilization Operations
    Military Assistance
    Humanitarian Relief
    Guarantee and Denial of Movement

PEACE ENFORCEMENT

    Enforcement of Sanctions
    Direct Intervention (to restore peace by the threat, or the actual use, of force)

The lists of tasks described within the above categories are not exhaustive but serve to depict the types of military activity that might be carried out. As the descriptions show, peacekeeping and Wider Peacekeeping are closely connected and overlapping activities. Peace enforcement, on the other hand, involves a predisposition to use force and implies the identification of an enemy. Force levels and structures deployed for peacekeeping (including Wider Peacekeeping) are unlikely to be appropriate for peace enforcement.

7.   *Scope and Level*. In covering Wider Peacekeeping this manual sets out doctrine at the tactical (ie field operations) level for UN-mandated multinational military operations covering the broader aspects of peacekeeping which, post Cold War, are receiving greater emphasis than hitherto. Peace enforcement lies outside the scope of this manual. A glossary of terms relating to Peace Support Operations is at Annex C.

SECTION FOUR - ORGANIZATION OF THE UN

8.   *Security Council*. The Security Council now consists of 5 permanent members (USA, Russia, UK, France and China) and 10 non-permanent members, half of which are elected each year by the General Assembly for a term of 2 years. The UN Charter confers on the Security Council unique authority to investigate any situation or conflict which threatens international peace and security. It is the only organization in the world that conveys legal authority for the use of force or intervention against a sovereign state. In carrying out these duties the Security Council acts on behalf of all UN members. The Security Council will usually task the Secretary General to prepare a plan to deal with the problem and will normally be the approving authority for that plan. If Security Council members cannot agree on a draft resolution (through lack of a requisite majority or through veto by a permanent member), they can (through a procedural vote which is not subject to veto) refer the matter to the UN General Assembly for consideration. The General Assembly itself, however, has no powers to authorize enforcement of the peace under Chapter VII of the UN Charter. Such powers are the exclusive preserve of the UN Security Council.

9. *Secretary General.* The UN Secretary General is responsible to the Security Council for the organization, conduct and direction of UN peacekeeping operations. As well as preparing the operational plan and presenting it to the Security Council for approval, the Secretary General is, in effect, the Commander in Chief, responsible for conducting negotiations with host countries, parties to a conflict and contributing member states.

10. *General Assembly.* The General Assembly may consider any matter referred to it by the Security Council as well as those matters pertaining to the promotion of international cooperation, disarmament, trusteeship and human rights. Most of its resolutions are not binding. However, it is the General Assembly that approves and apportions the UN's budget including all costs related to peacekeeping operations.

11. *Military Staff Committee.* Article 47 of the UN Charter calls for the establishment of a Military Staff Committee, made up of the Chiefs of Staff of the permanent members of the Security Council, to advise and assist on all questions relating to the Security Council's military requirements for the maintenance of international peace and security. In practice the Military Staff Committee has not played the rôle envisaged by the Charter and has exerted no influence on UN peacekeeping operations.

12. *Secretariat.* The UN Secretariat is headed by the Secretary General and is the permanent organization responsible for the establishment, coordination and administration of peacekeeping operations. It is, in effect, the UN's civil service. The main focus for peacekeeping within the UN Secretariat is the Department of Peacekeeping Operations. A military adviser offers guidance to the Secretary General on military matters.

SECTION FIVE - OPERATION OF THE UNITED NATIONS

13. *Debate.* The Secretary General is responsible under Article 99 for bringing matters before the Security Council for its consideration. However, any state may also bring before the Council matters relating to questions of international peace and security. Items are subsequently debated by the Security Council and draft resolutions discussed. Most resolutions are now passed by consensus. The requisite majority is 9 out of 15, although the five permanent members of the Security Council retain the power to veto a resolution by a negative vote.

14. *Security Council Resolutions.* A Security Council resolution may authorize a peacekeeping or peace enforcement operation. The resolution or one of its successors may also require the Secretary General to prepare a plan to deal with the problem. The Secretary General will then be responsible for informal negotiations with member states to secure troop contributions and logistic support. The mandate for the operation will usually be fully described in the Secretary General's report and endorsed in the relevant Security Council resolution. It is the Security Council resolution which provides the international legal authority for the mission. The Secretary General's report on the operation in Liberia (UNOMIL) and

the text of the relevant Security Council resolution (866) are attached as examples at Annex B.

15. ***Selection of Key Appointments***. The Secretary General will usually, but not always, select the key appointments for the force. In most current missions, because of their complexity, the Secretary General will appoint a Special Representative (normally from career UN staff) as overall Head of Mission, supported by a Force Commander (a military officer from a nation not involved in the conflict) and a lead UN civil agency.

16. ***Deployment***. Deployment is a UN responsibility but may be delegated to member states. Upon arrival in the area of operations, the national contingents will be placed under the operational control of the force commander. Prior to deployment a Status Of Forces Agreement (SOFA) should be agreed with the host nation. The SOFA will establish the legal position of a peacekeeping force and its members with the government and citizens of the host country. If a SOFA has not been concluded, the UN soldier will be covered by the UN Convention on Privileges and Immunities.

17. ***Chain of Command***. The operational chain of command for UN peacekeeping operations will be from the Force Commander to the Head of Mission (if not himself the Force Commander) to the Secretary General, who will in turn report to the Security Council. On a day-to-day basis, the Head of Mission will report to the Department of Peacekeeping Operations. National command links will need to be carefully managed so as not to inhibit operational effectiveness.

18. ***Regional Arrangements***. The UN Charter does not preclude regional arrangements or agencies contributing to the maintenance of international peace and security by taking the initiative to procure pacific settlements to local disputes within their regions. Indeed, Article 52 of the Charter encourages them to do so. The Charter, however, does stipulate that such organizations and their activities should be consistent with the purposes and principles of the UN. It is incumbent upon regional organizations not to use enforcement action to settle disputes without the prior authorization of the Security Council. Many regional organizations have been active in the past and an increase in their future involvement can be expected. Such organizations include the North Atlantic Treaty Organization, the Conference on Security and Cooperation in Europe, the Confederation of Independent States in the former Soviet Union, the Organization of American States, the Arab League, and the Organization of African Unity.

SECTION SIX - PEACEKEEPING DURING THE COLD WAR

19. The conflict of interests and hostility between East and West in the years after the Second World War limited the executive functions of the Security Council whenever an issue arose which was perceived to threaten the vital interests of one of its permanent members. The Security Council, then, as now, was unable to act if any of its permanent members vetoed a resolution or if the resolution did not receive the requisite number of votes. Consequently, the UN's pursuit of international

peace and security (with some notable exceptions - for example Korea and the latter stages of the Congo operation) did not often include provision for significant enforcement measures.

20. Throughout the period of the Cold War, the commitment of UN peacekeeping missions was usually subject, theoretically at least, to the following conditions:

> The support of the international community (represented by the Security Council).

> The continued existence of an ongoing political peace process.

> The consent of the parties to the conflict.

> An attitude of complete impartiality towards the belligerents.

> The minimum use of force, usually only in self-defence but which extended to the protection of the mandate.

> Financial approval for the mission from the General Assembly.

Under these conditions, UN peacekeeping contingents were usually armed and equipped only for self-defence. Peacekeeping was required to fulfil a delicate diplomatic rôle in gaining the influence and cooperation of the parties involved. Its success was largely dependent upon such cooperation.

SECTION SEVEN - A CHANGED SECURITY ENVIRONMENT

21. Throughout the period of the Cold War 30 million people were killed in more than 80 wars and conflicts. However, the competitive interests of the prevailing superpowers sometimes served to contain and suppress nationalist and inter-ethnic violence. Indeed, the superpowers were often able to cooperate over peacekeeping ventures. However, the demise of the Warsaw Pact in 1990 and the Soviet Union in 1991 brought an end to superpower competition and the Cold War conflict. As a result the international security environment, although remaining violent, changed. The removal of regional superpower interests and ideological pressures allowed new conflicts to emerge, often characterized by the fragmentation of former sovereign states and frequently based on intractable national, religious or ethnic differences, rooted in disputes of ancient historical origin. These conflicts were fuelled by the ready availability of large quantities of modern weaponry. In many areas of the world violence, even genocide, has been allowed to prevail unchecked.

SECTION EIGHT - WIDER PEACEKEEPING

22. *New Opportunities*. As well as unleashing restraints on communal violence, the ending of superpower competition introduced a greater degree of consensus to the UN Security Council. The effect of this was evinced in a new determination of the

Permanent Five as a group to solve breakdowns in international peace and security. This resolve was articulated in the UN Secretary General's report published in 1992 entitled 'An Agenda For Peace' which set out recommendations on how the capacity of the UN for preventive diplomacy, peacemaking and peacekeeping might be strengthened. The UN is therefore able now to pursue international peace and security in ways that lay greater emphasis on the wider aspects of peacekeeping including such things as conflict prevention, supervision of elections and humanitarian relief. This developing emphasis on 'Wider Peace-keeping' has received broad support from the world community, often stimulated by penetrating media coverage of world-wide conflicts and associated human suffering.

23. ***Deeper Commitment***. World support is reflected in an increase in the number of UN operations that have been launched emphasizing the wider aspects of traditional peacekeeping. In 1987, less than 10,000 troops were engaged in UN operations - by August 1993 this figure had increased to 76,000 by which time the UN had mounted as many missions in that intervening period as it had in the previous forty-three years of its existence. An historical record of selected UN operations that fall into the Wider Peacekeeping category is set out in the Supplement to this manual.

24. ***Characteristics***. Wider Peacekeeping operations are likely to take place in environments that display some or all of the following characteristics:

Numerous parties to a conflict.

Undisciplined factions (not responsive to their own controlling author-ities).

An ineffective ceasefire.

The absence of law and order.

Gross violations of human rights.

Risk of local armed opposition to UN forces.

The presence and involvement of large numbers of civilian organisa-tions, both government and non-government organisations (NGOs).

Collapse of civil infrastructure.

The presence of large numbers of refugees and displaced persons.

An undefined area of operations.

Wider Peacekeeping Operations are thus likely to occur in environments that bear the characteristics of civil war or insurgency. The grievances of parties to the conflict may have origins that are barely comprehensible to outsiders. Belligerent tactics might be improvised, irregular, irrational and bizarre including the use of environmental warfare (for example the firing of oil wells or emptying of chemical plants into water supplies). Random atrocity and large-scale human suffering may characterize the overall security environment. The intensity of such conflicts will probably vary from area to area and day to day. Changes in intensity could be rapid and unexpected. Local governments may be uncooperative or rendered ineffective and Wider Peacekeeping forces could face unexpected responsibilities in providing infrastructure facilities for the local populace in conditions of chaos.

25. **Spectrum of Tasks**. The spectrum of possible military tasks required in Wider Peacekeeping operations is broad and will often apply to an unstable, dangerous environment. Such operations could be mandated under Chapter VI or VII of the UN Charter. In certain circumstances a reinforced military presence might be required with contingent heavy weapons, indirect fire support and reserves. It is likely that the commitment of a Wider Peacekeeping force to an operational theatre would often be made after the situation had passed the critical point at which it might be readily managed, thus compounding the difficulties and risks faced by those committed.

26. **Sponsorship**. Wider Peacekeeping operations will most likely be joint, multinational (with allied or coalition forces) and multiagency. They will almost certainly be sponsored under the aegis of the UN, possibly through regional organizations and agencies or under the leadership of a member state.

27. **Coherence and Coordination**. It is highly likely that there will be many governmental and non-governmental organisations (NGO's) operating in the wider peacekeeping theatre. If the causes of the conflict, both humanitarian and political are to be effectively addressed the military, political and humanitarian activities of all the involved organisations, both military and civilian will need be coordinated in a single 'campaign' plan. The production of the 'campaign' plan is the responsibility of the Head of Mission, the Special Representative of the Secretary General, (SRSG). This 'campaign' plan should clearly define objectives and their sequencing, allocate resources, responsibilities, tasks and main effort, and establish inter-organisational relationships' and coordination mechanisms. It will have to take especial account of the different professional cultures and working practices of those involved. NGOs can only be coordinated by consent, not direction.

SECTION NINE - DEFINING SUCCESS

28. Wider Peacekeeping conflicts will require resolution by conciliation rather than termination by force. Thus, as in peacekeeping, military operations will be designed principally to create or support the conditions in which political and diplomatic activities may proceed. As in other OOTW military action cannot, therefore, be viewed as an end in itself, but will rather complement diplomatic, economic and humanitarian endeavours which together will pursue political

objectives. Success will thus be measured by the rate at which the sum total of those activities progresses towards the achievement of the UN mandate. The concept of victory or defeat is therefore inappropriate to Wider Peacekeeping operations. The subordination of operations to political and diplomatic activity may result in shifting and incoherent military objectives - a frustration that may often be faced by military personnel and which will require considerable efforts by military commanders to manage. In any event the activities and methods used by the UN force will be constrained absolutely by the scope of its mandate and the demands of international law.

CHAPTER TWO

CONCEPTUAL APPROACH

"A peace is of the nature of a conquest;
For then both parties nobly are subdued,
And neither party loser."
> William Shakespeare

SECTION ONE - INTRODUCTION

1. ***Conceptual Approach***. A valid conceptual approach must frame a proper understanding of Wider Peacekeeping. Without such an approach, analysis and instruction will be flawed - and wrong lessons will be taught. A legitimate conceptual approach to Wider Peacekeeping should identify key doctrinal determinants and lead to the development of a sound, balanced and effective doctrine which will allow readers to assess for themselves the foundation of the doctrine that follows and also to understand what lies behind its overall emphasis. This chapter therefore seeks to describe the conceptual approach to Wider Peacekeeping from which is derived the remaining doctrine in this manual.

> **CONTENTS**
>
> INTRODUCTION
>
> PRAGMATIC AND HISTORICAL PERSPECTIVES
>
> THE SIGNIFICANCE OF CONSENT
>
> MANAGING CONSENT
>
> IMPARTIALITY
>
> THE USE OF FORCE
>
> ASSESSMENT AND APPLICATIONS
>
> SUMMARY

2. ***Wider Peacekeeping Tasks***. The categories of Wider Peacekeeping tasks were listed in Chapter One and are described in more detail below:

   a. *Conflict Prevention* is an activity that seeks to anticipate and forestall conflict. It embraces early warning, surveillance, stabilizing measures and preventive deployment. The latter is likely to require large scale deployments backed up by a substantial reinforcement and support capability.

   b. *Demobilization Operations* describe the controlled withdrawal, demobilization and rehabilitation of belligerents. Something that in this context would be carried out with the prior agreement of the parties concerned.

   c. *Military Assistance* refers to all forms of mandated military assistance rendered by a Wider Peacekeeping force to a foreign civil authority and refers to such things as supervising a transfer of power, reforming security forces and developing or supporting civil infrastructure facilities. The maintenance of law and order is foundational to such activity.

d.   *Humanitarian Relief* operations seek to meet the needs of residents, refugees or displaced persons. They may be conducted independently by the military or in support of aid agencies. They are likely to involve such things as the protection of supply deliveries and relief workers, and the establishment, support and protection of safe havens. Such operations may also include administrative, coordination and logistical activities to support humanitarian relief efforts.

e.   *Guarantee and Denial of Movement* describes those operations that are mandated to guarantee or deny movement by air, land, or sea in particular areas and over certain routes. Such operations may be mounted to allow ships to pass through a threatened sea lane, or to enable aircraft to reach a besieged city or community. The denial of movement usually focuses on the establishment of no-fly zones over a specified region or community. Operations to guarantee and deny movement normally involve the coordinated presence of warships and combat aircraft. As such they are usually controlled at the operational or strategic level. Accordingly, they will not be considered in detail in this tactical level manual.

The above categories, covering the gamut of Wider Peacekeeping tasks, are neither exhaustive, exclusive nor self-contained. The activities described will often occur simultaneously and overlap. However, for doctrinal purposes the categories serve to provide a useful framework for consideration. They are described in greater detail in Chapter Three.

SECTION TWO - PRAGMATIC AND HISTORICAL PERSPECTIVES

3.   ***Pragmatism***. The British Army has a reputation of pragmatism in its approach to operations. Its flexibility and high standards of training have traditionally enabled it to adopt realistic approaches to the task in hand - approaches that can be made to work. The first stage in developing doctrine for Wider Peacekeeping operations is therefore to assess, from a military point of view, how best such tasks might be done. Analysis of the tasks themselves, the range of environments in which the tasks might be undertaken, and lessons learned by practitioners generally point in the same direction. The most common conclusion of such assessments indicates that the practical demands of the tasks require a significant degree of local cooperation. Such cooperation, of course, depends on the presence of consent. Peacekeepers are most likely to succeed if they are able to convince the belligerent factions of a link between compliance and mutual advantage and when all concerned have something to gain from participation in the peace process or something to lose if they do not. Wider Peacekeeping

> "... The UN peacekeeping plan is not viable until various local authorities extend the necessary cooperation ..."
>
> **UN Secretary General**
>
> (briefing the Security Council on UNPROFOR)

operations cannot succeed in the face of entrenched, widespread opposition. Forcible pacification is not possible with the level of resources normally allocated to a peacekeeping operation. Nor would forcible pacification necessarily provide a long term solution to the conflict. A pragmatic evaluation of peacekeeping operations indicates that a significant degree of local cooperation is necessary for any prospect of lasting success. This assessment has been recognized and is understood within the UN. At a lower level, this same understanding is reflected in the British Army's assessments:

---

1 CHESHIRES BOSNIA POST OPERATION REPORT

"... LOs were deployed ... to begin the development of a framework of trust and confidence that was to prove fundamental to the success of the Group's mission ..."

"The concept of a framework of confidence and trust based on the establishing of relationships between the local military, political and civil personalities and the Battalion Group ... remained the key to executing the mission ... It was these personal relationships which underwrote the ability of the 1 CHESHIRE Group to be pro-active in its concept of operations ..."

"The resolving of or attempted mediation in local and national inter-ethnic disputes was a major part of the Battalion Group's efforts ..."

"The conduct of negotiation ... required enormous restraint and patience ..."

---

4.   ***Pragmatic Principles and Operational Techniques***. The pragmatic requirement for local cooperation (deriving from consent) consistently emphasizes the necessity of building a framework of confidence and trust, and observing principles such as impartiality and minimum force that develop and sustain consent. Operational techniques such as negotiation, mediation and the use of civil affairs programmes ('hearts and minds') are important for the same reason. Such principles and operational techniques are, in effect, those that were applied to peacekeeping during the Cold War years - backing up the practical analysis of Wider Peacekeeping tasks which repeatedly emphasizes the necessity of continuing to observe them. In undertaking operations of this kind, therefore, pragmatism evidently demands the application of traditional peacekeeping principles - principles aimed at promoting and sustaining cooperation and consent. The risks entailed and force levels required of an approach that dispenses with a broad consensual framework renders impractical most operations that might be mounted in a Wider Peacekeeping context.

5.   ***History***. History provides collateral for the conclusions reached by the pragmatic assessments described above. A study of previous peacekeeping operations shows that the wider aspects of peacekeeping described in Paragraph 2 are not new. Most of the Wider Peacekeeping tasks have already been done during the Cold War under the label of peacekeeping. Such operations appear to be part and

parcel of Cold War peacekeeping - not so much in the British Army's experience with the UN - but certainly in the UN's experience at large, as well as in the experience of other peacekeeping operations conducted by national and multinational bodies.

PEACEKEEPING DURING THE COLD WAR

CONFLICT PREVENTION
UNFICYP (Cyprus, 1964-)
UNEF I & II (Egypt & Sinai, 1956-79)
UNDOF (Golan Heights, 1974)
UNMOGIP (Kashmir, 1949-)
DOMREP (Dominican Republic 1965-66)
UNTSO (Palestine, 1948-)

HUMANITARIAN RELIEF
UNIFIL (Lebanon, 1978-)
*ADF (Lebanon, 1976-83)
ONUC (Congo, 1960-64)
UNFICYP (Cyprus, 1964-)

GUARANTEE & DENIAL
OF MOVEMENT
ONUC (Congo, 1960-64)
UNFICYP (Cyprus, 1964-)
UNEF II (Suez Canal & Sinai, 1973-79)

DEMOBILIZATION OPERATIONS
UNTSO (Palestine, 1948-)
UNEF I & II (Egypt & Sirai, 1956-79)
ONUC (Congo, 1960-64)
UNIPOM (India & Pakistan, 1965-66)
UNDOF (Golan Heights, 1974-)
*CMF (Rhodesia/Zimbabwe, 1979-80)

MILITARY ASSISTANCE
ONUC (Congo, 1960-64)
UNSF & UNTEA (West Irian, 1962-63)
UNFICYP (Cyprus, 1964-)
*MNF I & II (Beirut, 1982-84)
*CMF (Rhodesia/Zimbabwe, 1979-80)
UNIFIL (Lebanon, 1978-)
*ADF (Lebanon, 1976-83)

* = Non-UN operations

Of course there are differences post Cold War, not least in the scale, participation and hybrid nature of such operations, involving as they do large numbers of government and non-governmental agencies. More often, too, the environment in which these tasks are done is volatile and prone to escalation in violence. Such operations are therefore likely to require professional, well-trained, well-equipped armies prepared for rapid and unexpected transitions in the nature and intensity of activity. However, the intrinsic nature of Wider Peacekeeping tasks seems not to be unique and differs little from the nature of what has gone before. It appears, therefore, that the Wider Peacekeeping tasks post Cold War do not reflect a novel development, but rather a changing emphasis in terms of scale, participation and involvement. Such operations have, for the British Army, become more prominent post Cold War.

6.   ***Context***. Pragmatism and history thus seem to place Wider Peacekeeping tasks firmly within the peacekeeping category - a category where the preservation of consent is a principal guide of operational activity. To place them in some fresh category appears not only specious historically, but misleading doctrinally since it would imply that such things as popular support, the conduct of negotiation, mediation and conciliation and the building of confidence and cooperation mattered less post Cold War and that peacekeeping principles might be safely abandoned in favour of a doctrine more orientated towards warfighting which took little or no account of the need to preserve consent. Such an approach would offer little chance of practical success.

SECTION THREE - THE SIGNIFICANCE OF CONSENT

7. ***Peacekeeping and Peace Enforcement***. Peacekeeping (and within that category, Wider Peacekeeping) must be set within the overall framework of peace support operations - particularly with regard to peace enforcement. Doctrinally, Wider Peacekeeping can only be analyzed coherently if it is considered in this wider context.

8. ***Categories***. Chapter One describes peacekeeping, Wider Peacekeeping and peace enforcement as follows:

    a. *Peacekeeping*. Operations carried out with the consent of the belligerent parties in support of efforts to achieve or maintain peace in order to promote security and sustain life in areas of potential or actual conflict.

    b. *Wider Peacekeeping*. The wider aspects of peacekeeping operations carried out with the general consent of the belligerent parties but in an environment that may be highly volatile.

    c. *Peace Enforcement*. Operations carried out to restore peace between belligerent parties who do not all consent to intervention and who may be engaged in combat activities.

    Wider Peacekeeping is thus classified as an element of peacekeeping. Using these descriptions, therefore, two basic categories of activity are identified: peacekeeping (including Wider Peacekeeping) and peace enforcement.

9. ***Differential of Consent***. The above descriptions (similar in substance to US definitions, and compatible with those of most nations) draw out the distinguishing criterion of consent. Peacekeeping and Wider Peacekeeping rely on having the consent of the belligerent parties, at least at the operational (ie theatre) level, and depend for their success on consent-promoting techniques - peace enforcement does not. What divides peacekeeping from peace enforcement, therefore, is not the level of violence, but the level of consent.

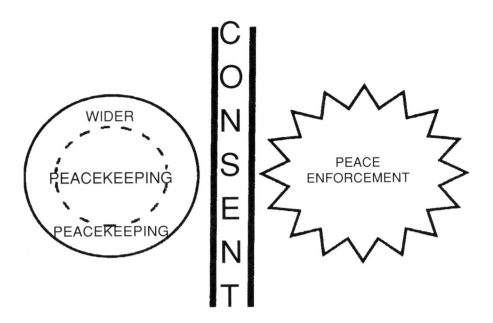

Consent thus emerges as the fundamental and key differential. Its identification is borne out both by the pragmatic analysis of Wider Peacekeeping tasks and a historical assessment of Cold War peacekeeping. For Wider Peacekeeping therefore, consent is confirmed as foundational to any prospect of long-term success. Lessons learned reports have highlighted the point that seeking to promote and sustain consent is the most important activity in which the tactical commander can engage. The history of peacekeeping has consistently shown that consent is the only effective vehicle for carrying peacekeeping operations forward.

10. **Nature of Consent.** Consent to Wider Peacekeeping activities is likely to be anything but absolute. In theatre, depending on the volatility of the general environment, it is unlikely ever to be more than partial and could amount to nothing more than tolerance of presence. Consent is something that the peacekeeper can expect to have bits of, from certain people, in certain places, for certain things, for certain periods of time. When viewed in close-up, the consent divide between peacekeeping and peace enforcement might be depicted as follows:

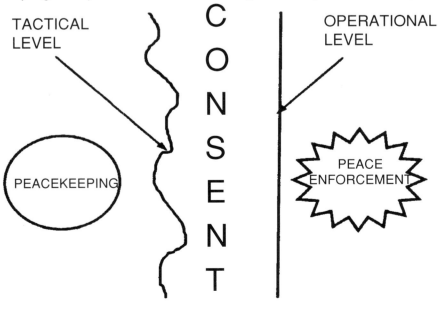

Consent at the tactical (field operations) level will derive from local events and prevailing popular opinion. It will be subject to frequent change and its boundary will therefore be mobile and poorly defined. At the operational (ie theatre) level, consent will devolve largely from formal agreements and that boundary will consequently be relatively clear-cut and easier to discern.

SECTION FOUR - MANAGING CONSENT

11. **Transmission of Consent**. Lessons learned reports have also highlighted the need for continual effort to transmit consent between the operational and tactical levels. For example, if the theatre commander has secured the agreement of a faction leader to a particular course of action, he should then do everything he can to have that agreement transmitted down to those faction members facing his tactical commanders in the field. Similarly, one of the most useful peacekeeping commodities that a tactical commander can pass back to his superiors are the fruits of agreement made with local faction leaders, especially those which build on and reinforce previously negotiated agreements .

12. **Cooperative Ventures**. Consent will be further promoted if the parties to a conflict can be endowed with vested interests in successfully resolving their own dispute. If the belligerents can somehow be made shareholders of the peace process, then their motivation to cooperate will be greatly increased. At the tactical level, this possibility may be pursued by creating incentive-based opportunities for competing factions to cooperate together in jointly carrying out certain Wider Peacekeeping tasks. Such action would be risky and difficult but, as another dimension of consent-promoting possibilities, deserves consideration.

13. **Threats to Consent**. Once the nature and requirement for consent has been identified as the crucial differential between peacekeeping and peace enforcement, a valid approach to peacekeeping requires that differential to be interpreted doctrinally. If a peacekeeping force is introduced into a conflict situation with the consent of the different parties to the conflict, it is clear that operational conduct should seek to preserve that consensual divide. There are various ways that the consent barrier might be inadvertently breached.

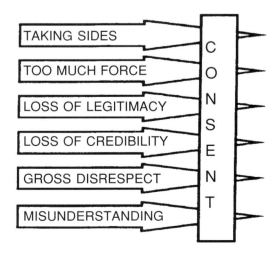

If, for example, the peacekeeping force should abandon its impartial status and take sides, it would reduce its status to that of one of the parties to the conflict, losing its credibility and prejudicing its ability to control what is going on. In effect, the force would join the conflict and become part of the problem it was there to resolve. A crass, unfocused use of force would be similarly liable to breach the consent divide.

14. ***Guarding Consent.*** Critical principles, therefore, which will guard against crossing the consent barrier are depicted below:

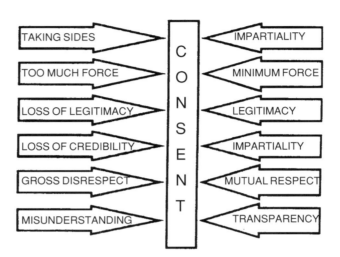

The ability of the peacekeeping force to contribute to conflict resolution depends upon the exercise of the principles shown above which will protect its third party referee status. Such status is key to the force's self-protection. Consent is thus supported by the following principles:

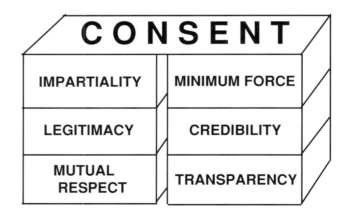

SECTION FIVE - IMPARTIALITY

15. ***Importance of Impartiality.*** Of the principles listed above, impartiality, deriving from and, in turn, sustaining consent, has the widest and most significant application. An analogy serves to illustrate the importance of impartiality to Wider Peacekeeping. In a game of rugby the referee's legitimacy and third party status are guaranteed by the rules and

the player's acceptance of the rules. As such he is able to control the course of the game and act as the supreme adjudicator between the opposing sides. On the field the referee is outnumbered 30:1 and he stands no chance of exerting his will by force. What enables him to control the players is the perceived legitimacy of his status. A key ingredient of that legitimacy is his impartiality. If the impartial, third party element of his status as a legitimate authority is lost, he loses control of the game, the players start brawling and his personal safety may eventually be in jeopardy.

16. **Nature of Impartiality**. The concept of impartiality thus emerges as a major determinant of the conduct of peacekeeping operations. That said, impartiality should not be regarded as too exact or absolute a commodity. Just as consent is likely to be incomplete, so the concept of impartiality is likely to prove inexact and fragmentary in practice. It must be appreciated too that impartiality is as much a product of perception as of practice. It is not enough for the peacekeeper to act impartially. He must be seen to be acting impartially and that perspective, including transparent motives and the avoidance of all possible scope for misunderstanding, should be an important consideration in conducting peacekeeping and Wider Peacekeeping operations. In practice it is likely that most factions will accuse the Wider Peacekeeping force of being prejudiced against them. As long as the commander can refute such accusations and continues to operate in a demonstrably even-handed fashion, the impartiality principle can be upheld.

SECTION SIX - THE USE OF FORCE

17. **Introduction**. Judgements concerning the use of force are likely to be the most critical that a commander will make. The unrestricted use of force in a Wider Peacekeeping operation is likely to cross the consent divide faster than anything else. The misuse of force risks destabilizing peacekeeping operations and causing an uncontrolled and violent transition to peace enforcement.

18. **Criterion of Consent**. The identification of the critical consent divide allows the use of force to be addressed in a way that takes full account of its wider connotations. The need to preserve overall consent does not foreclose the use of force by peacekeepers. Indeed, majority consent may serve to marginalize a minority withholding consent and render it vulnerable to the use of force. If a strong consensual framework reduces the status of armed opposition to that of maverick banditry, then demonstrably reasonable and proportionate force may be employed against it without fear of fracturing the consent divide.

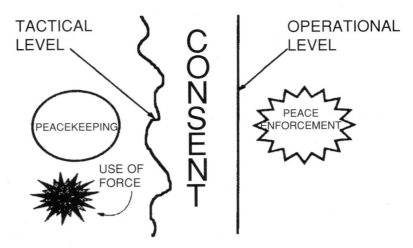

For this reason, the use of force may represent a valid consensual peacekeeping technique. Consent can thus facilitate, not hinder the use of force. It may be that force has to be used in a way that breaches the tactical edge of the consent divide:

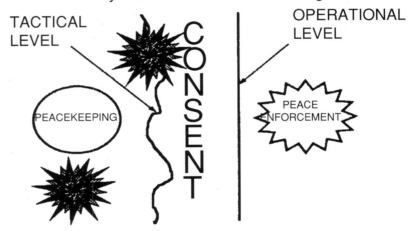

In such circumstances, stability may be retained if the operational boundary to the consent divide is preserved intact - the consent of faction leaders at theatre level may serve to contain local upset. The use of force in such a way, although dangerous, is therefore not necessarily fatal to the overall stability of the peacekeeping operation. If, however, force is used in a way that breaches both the tactical and operational levels of consent - then destabilization and a transition to peace enforcement becomes a serious likelihood:

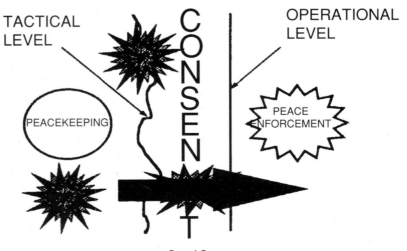

The challenge for the Wider Peacekeeping is to create a framework of consent that is sufficiently robust so as to withstand the measured use of force. Such considerations should guide the formulation of doctrine concerning the use of force.

19. ***Impartiality***. The principle of impartiality will also offer guidance on whether and how force might be employed. For example, force may be used impartially in large measure to protect a humanitarian convoy. However, the deliberate targetting or arming of particular factions would clearly abandon impartiality since it would deliberately penalise or favour particular parties to the conflict. Such action would cross the consent divide with all the consequences that are likely to follow.

20. ***Doctrinal Requirement***. Wider Peacekeeping doctrine emphasises therefore that the consequences of using force reach far beyond the immediate tactical situation. Many aspects require consideration besides Rules of Engagement. The doctrine requires that the use of force takes account of its long term effects. Commanders need critical principles to guide their use of force and also be made aware of alternatives to its use. Doctrine for the use of force is covered in Chapter Four.

SECTION SEVEN - ASSESSMENT AND APPLICATIONS

21. ***A Model***. Thus far, therefore, analysis offers a conceptual approach to PeaceSupport Operations based on the following model:

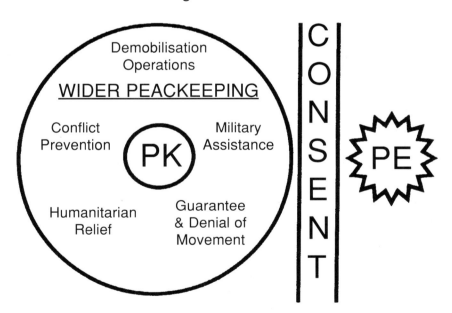

On the left is peacekeeping, embracing those Wider Peacekeeping aspects described earlier. On the right is peace enforcement. Separating them both is consent.

22. ***The Tightrope***. The gamut of Peace Support Operations might therefore be likened to the performance of a tightrope walker at a circus. In peacekeeping the

performer carries only a balancing pole and there is a hushed and respectful silence in the crowd (reflecting the unquestioning consent of the parties to the conflict) as the performer walks the tightrope. In Wider Peacekeeping operations the performer carries the same balancing pole and walks the identical tightrope. He also has the general consent of the parties to the conflict. However, on this occasion it is apparent that not everyone approves of his performance and the circus audience is restive and noisy. Some individuals are even throwing missiles at the tightrope walker as he makes his journey.

23. ***Doctrinal Approaches***. The tightrope analogy illustrates the understanding that Wider Peacekeeping is an element of peacekeeping. The former represents, in effect, the more challenging aspects of the latter. Peacekeeping and Wider Peacekeeping depend upon maintaining a framework of consent by observing those principles which promote and sustain consent - in particular, impartiality and minimum force. The Wider Peacekeeping environment is volatile and risky and requires a highly professional commitment, but the intrinsic nature of Wider Peacekeeping is that of peacekeeping and demands a doctrinal approach that honours the same principles, though the soldier is likely to have to call on many of his battle skills in the process.

24. ***The Purpose of Wider Peacekeeping Doctrine***. It is clear therefore that there is a distinction between Wider Peacekeeping and peace enforcement. The distinction is derived from the presence or absence of consent and is further defined by the differing military approaches to operations in the two categories. But there is one additional and fundamental point to make in this context. The purpose of this doctrine is to provide guidance not only on how to conduct a Wider Peacekeeping operation but also, crucially, how to prevent it slipping by default into peace enforcement. That slippage will occur when the consent divide has been crossed - in other words when one or more parties to the conflict no longer give their tacit consent to the presence and activities of the peacekeeper.

25. ***The Consequences of Crossing the Consent Divide***. Case histories of multinational peacekeeping operations demonstrate the dangers of inadvertently crossing the consent boundary from peacekeeping to peace enforcement. The consequences of such a transition are depicted overleaf. If perceived to be taking sides or using force in a way that alienates support, the peacekeeping force loses its credibility as a trustworthy third party, thereby prejudicing its legitimacy and security. The force's resources will then become ever more devoted to protecting itself. If it actually joins the conflict it was put there to police it is likely to become embroiled in activities that are irrelevant to the overall campaign aim. Such a situation will almost certainly result in a loss of popular support, an attendant loss of control and unrestricted escalation in the level of violence which will heighten political tension and foreclose opportunities for resolving the conflict. The consent divide, if crossed by default may prove to have been a Rubicon. Once on the other side, there may be very little chance of getting back and the only way out for that particular force is likely to be by leaving the theatre.

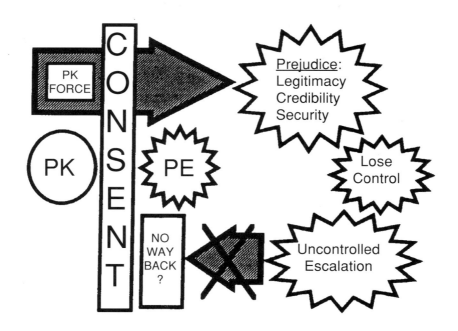

26. **Making Choices**. This is not to say that a UN force could not or should not undertake peace enforcement operations from the outset if that is demanded by analysis of the mission and conditions on the ground. Nor is it to suggest that a deployed Wider Peacekeeping contingent would necessarily be unable to transit to such operations. Transiting to peace enforcement, however, should be a deliberate, pre-meditated act, taking account of the risks involved, and matched by appropriate force levels, equipments, and doctrine. It would, for instance, require substantial force restructuring and redeployment, the evacuation of unarmed monitors and civilian workers, and the probable termination of humanitarian operations. The overlay of close air support on a peacekeeping force will not of itself, therefore, be sufficient preparation for transition to peace enforcement. The choice should be made, at the outset, of which course of action is going to be followed. Once that political decision has been taken, then practitioners on the ground must act consistently with it. Since the Wider Peacekeeping operational environment is, however, likely to be complicated, violent and volatile, the danger of inadvertently crossing the consent divide may often be present. In such circumstances, there will frequently be temptations to mix the two approaches. Wider Peacekeeping doctrine, however, seeks to identify and guard against this danger.

SECTION EIGHT - SUMMARY

27. **Summary**. This Chapter has described the conceptual approach to the doctrine of Wider Peacekeeping. The practical necessity and historical precedent for a consensual framework to such operations has been highlighted. The significance and nature of consent as the doctrinal divide separating peacekeeping (including Wider Peacekeeping) from the high risk and resource-intensive activity of peace enforcement has been identified as an inexact but critical divide that should only

be crossed deliberately and after careful preparation. Care should be taken to avoid actions (such as an indiscriminate use of force) that risk an accidental drift across the consent divide. Wider Peacekeeping doctrine should therefore clearly identify the consent barrier and emphasize the importance of seeking to stay within it, drawing attention to those principles that guard against its breach. The nature of the consent divide has important implications for the use of force.

28. **Comment**. Doctrine for Wider Peacekeeping therefore has its focus on the significance of consent and its utility as a determinant of operational conduct. Activities that breach the consent differential should not be undertaken in a Wider Peacekeeping campaign. Such inconsistency of approach could set at risk the entire framework for operations. In practice, Wider Peacekeeping operations are likely to represent a continual struggle to preserve and sustain whatever consensual framework might exist. Military techniques that have the greatest utility are likely to be those that address perceptions directly and promote and develop consent. The content and emphasis of the Wider Peacekeeping doctrine described in this manual derives from this overall conceptual approach.

29. **Overview**. The crucial elements of Wider Peacekeeping doctrine might be depicted as shown as follows:

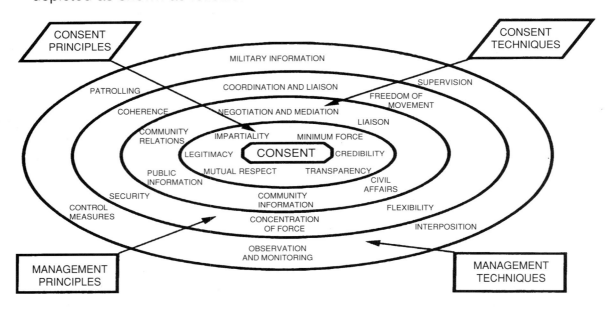

The goal of consent lies at the heart of Wider Peacekeeping doctrine. The inner ring of principles and outer ring of techniques are those that address perceptions directly, thus preserving, sustaining and developing consent. The physical management techniques depicted on the outer rim derive their meaning only from what they enclose. Without understanding of that, the practice of such things as patrolling and interposition will represent little more doctrinally than the exterior of an empty shell. The conceptual approach to Wider Peacekeeping is thus predicated on the centrality of consent and the ultimate purpose that consent imparts to the principles and operational techniques described. It is in the application of these principles, and in the employment of the operational techniques that support them, that the key to successful peacekeeping in the future lies.

CHAPTER THREE

OPERATIONAL TASKS

"The arms are fair, when the intent of bearing them is just."
William Shakespeare

SECTION ONE - INTRODUCTION

1.   Chapter Two described the following categories of Wider Peacekeeping operations:

Conflict Prevention
Demobilization Operations
Military Assistance
Humanitarian Relief
Guarantee and Denial of Movement

These categories, however, may not capture every form of military activity in Wider Peacekeeping operations and should not be regarded as exhaustive. Nor should the categories be considered discrete since they will often overlap and the military activities required by one category may be common to others. Nevertheless, the categories represent a useful framework for the examination of the characteristics, requirements and practice of Wider Peacekeeping tasks and their associated military activities.

> CONTENTS
>
> INTRODUCTION
>
> CONFLICT PREVENTION
>
> DEMOBILIZATION OPERATIONS
>
> MILITARY ASSISTANCE
>
> HUMANITARIAN RELIEF
>
> GUARANTEE AND DENIAL OF MOVEMENT

SECTION TWO - CONFLICT PREVENTION

INTRODUCTION

2.   The maxim "prevention is better than cure" has always been true of classic peacekeeping operations. In this context, preventive measures have traditionally relied on and exploited the consent of all parties concerned, the existence of an established ceasefire and the presence of an effective political framework to complement peacekeeping activities. Preventive measures are also possible in Wider Peacekeeping operations, although in this instance they are likely to take place in conditions where, despite an overall consensual framework, belligerent parties may not be responsive to their own central controls and consequently uncooperative. Sporadic outbreaks of violence might be taking place, Wider Peacekeeping forces may face local armed opposition, and there may be no effective state government. The prevention of conflict in such operations may require large scale deployments backed up by a substantial reinforcement and support capability. There are four complementary Wider Peacekeeping activities that contribute to the prevention of conflict or the resurgence of hostilities:

Early warning.
Surveillance.
Stabilizing measures.
Preventive deployment.

With the exception of EW activity each can be applied at all levels of military operations.

EARLY WARNING

3.   Early warning is essentially a strategic or operational level activity and is the product of an effective information system. Operations conducted at the tactical level, however, may have an important contribution to make to early warning. By identifying the threat of an outbreak or escalation of violence early warning will buy time for a range of preventive diplomatic and military actions to be effected. Commanders must therefore focus their military information assets on any potential crisis situation within their areas of operation. Resources should be set aside for this specific purpose. Surveillance activity (covered below) will contribute to the accomplishment of this task.

SURVEILLANCE

4.   The presence of widespread and impartial surveillance in an area of operation will deter breaches of the peace by parties to a conflict. In the first place surveillance will remove the element of surprise from actions that the parties or their enemies might take, especially if it is known that the information arising from the surveillance is shared with all concerned. The loss of surprise will greatly improve the opportunity for the force to anticipate offensive action by the parties to a conflict, thus degrading the effectiveness of aggression and making such action seem less worthwhile. Secondly, effective surveillance will disclose to the international community culpability that might arise from actions which belligerents may be tempted to take. In each case, the likelihood of aggression being rewarded is lessened, and the threat of anticipatory responses by Wider Peacekeeping forces, or indeed an opposing party, is heightened. Effective surveillance is therefore a key conflict prevention measure. Full use should be made of the entire range of techniques and equipment available including observation, monitoring and patrols (covered in Chapter Five), and attended and unattended electronic, optical and acoustic surveillance devices.

STABILIZING MEASURES

5.   Stabilizing measures will contribute to the lowering of tension in an area and, applied to the parties to a conflict, may take several forms:

Mutual and balanced reductions in personnel and equipments.
The establishment of demilitarized buffer zones.
Zonal restrictions on the deployment of weapons and manpower.
Advance reporting of military activities or exercises.

Joint inspections of disputed areas.
The exchange of liaison teams.

Such stabilizing measures can be applied at all levels and may represent the first steps towards negotiations for a political settlement. Communications between the parties involved in the conflict are essential for stabilisation. Shuttle diplomacy, an establishment of mutual trust between the Wider Peacekeeper and belligerents, the establishment and maintenance of local government and law and order are important elements of stability. This will be particularly relevant in the early stages of an operation when only a fragile peace may exist between the parties. Commanders should continually review the potential for implementing stabilizing measures at any level in their areas of operation.

PREVENTIVE DEPLOYMENT

6.   *Characteristics*. A preventive deployment in Wider Peacekeeping operations is likely to take place in an area of potential conflict either between states or within a state where tension is rising between factions. Although there will be consent to the deployment, a ceasefire or peace plan may not have been agreed and the situation may be characterized by sporadic outbreaks of violence and the possibility of local armed opposition to the deployment.

7.   *Nature*. Despite the belligerents' consent to the deployment a preventive deployment force generally relies on its strength and authority to deter violence and promote negotiation. Its primary rôle is thus the interpositional forestalling of armed aggression.   A preventive deployment force should therefore be armed for protective tasks that go beyond the demands of self-defence and should be enhanced by on-call reinforcements and support, perhaps in the form of indirect fire assets and air power. The security framework provided by preventive deployment will enable other Wider Peacekeeping functions to be discharged including early warning, surveillance, stabilizing measures, the protection of humanitarian relief and diplomatic activity to resolve the underlying political problem. The composition of a preventive deployment force may therefore include civil administrative personnel including police and relief workers. Survivability could also prove a critical factor and it would be unusual for the force's personnel not to have armoured protection for its duties.

8.   *Credibility*. Credibility is the key to success in preventive deployment. The force must therefore be strong enough, and plainly perceived to be so, to 'hold the ring' - if necessary until its reinforcements and support arrive. The reinforcement and support capacity should also be clearly communicated to the parties involved to promote the force's overall credibility. Once deployed, the force should conduct patrolling and other military activities so that its visibility and credibility remain high.

9.   *Scope*. A preventive deployment may be carried out at low level within the area of operations of a national contingent. At a higher, theatre-wide level, preventive deployment may be undertaken multinationally as a symbolic and actual commitment of the international community. At that level, the force may be enhanced by

the presence of an offshore or regional coalition strike force. At any level, preventive deployment may have to cope with rapid escalations in violence; where ultimate consent collapses it may even have to transition to peace enforcement.

SECTION THREE - DEMOBILIZATION OPERATIONS

INTRODUCTION

10. There is little chance of lasting peace without security. The nature of Wider Peacekeeping operations, therefore, is such as to require at least a rudimentary security framework as a precursor to further activity. Demobilization operations, representing in effect the implementation of negotiated settlements, are therefore a foundational military task in the Wider Peacekeeping context.

NATURE

11. Demobilization constitutes those actions taken by a Wider Peacekeeping force to restore and maintain a reasonable level of peace and security within a state or region. If fighting on a major scale is in progress, peace enforcement operations may be required which are outside the scope of this manual. In the Wider Peacekeeping context demobilization operations will depend on resolving rather than terminating the conflict. This cannot be achieved without obtaining a substantial level of popular support. Demobilization can take place at theatre or local level and commanders at all levels should continually review and exploit whatever opportunities they might have to carry out such operations.

CHARACTERISTICS

12. A Wider Peacekeeping force committed to demobilization operations is likely to encounter some or all of the following characteristics in the situation they find themselves:

   a.   An ill-defined and widespread area of operations wherein opposing factions may be inextricably mixed. Conflict may be inter or intra state.

   b.   Inter-communal violence and atrocity.

   c.   Several parties to the conflict, some of which may be hard to identify, undisciplined, lacking restraint and barely accountable to any central or recognized authority.

   d.   Sporadic local opposition to the Wider Peacekeeping force.

   e.   Widespread unmarked mines and residual ordnance restricting movement.

STAGES

13. There are numerous military tasks that contribute to demobilization. They are considered below in the context of the five main stages to the demobilization process:

Securing agreement
Establishing and managing a ceasefire
Withdrawal and assembly of belligerents
Disarming of belligerents
Dispersal and rehabilitation of belligerents

These stages need not necessarily take place on a theatre-wide basis. They may be adapted and implemented successively in local areas of operation. In essence, demobilization depends on establishing and sustaining a ceasefire. Subsequent stages depend on the ceasefire being maintained. Demobilization operations may offer opportunities for the Wider Peacekeeping force to delegate joint responsibilities to the belligerent parties. There is also likely to be scope for a considerable degree of cooperation and sharing of resources between the Wider Peacekeeping force and the parties to the conflict.

STAGE 1 - SECURING AGREEMENT

14. Securing appropriate prior agreement to demobilization operations is a necessary precursor to the Wider Peacekeeping force's further action. Such agreement will also constitute an important factor in the force's legitimacy. Depending on the level at which the operations are mounted, agreement may stem from anything ranging from a UN Security Council Resolution to a regional peace plan to negotiations brokered between local factions. The agreement should, if possible, be made with all parties concerned and should protect the freedom of movement of the Wider Peacekeeping force and include timetables for action. The agreement should focus on establishing and maintaining a ceasefire. Ideally, the agreements should also offer rewards and penalties to motivate compliance by hostile factions.

STAGE 2 - ESTABLISHING AND MANAGING A CEASEFIRE

15. *Scope*. The supervision of ceasefires has traditionally been associated with classic peacekeeping and has normally depended on a clear and agreed geographical delineation between two opposing factions. However, this may not always be the case and in the volatile environment of Wider Peacekeeping a literal ceasefire may prove impossible to achieve. In this situation, ceasefires should be understood as referring to the cessation of hostile activity.

16. *Delineated Ceasefires*. In geographical terms, a ceasefire may be delineated using the following elements:

    a. *Ceasefire Line*. The Ceasefire Line marks the forward limit of the positions occupied by opposing factions. It is, by its nature, usually the subject of contention - particularly when it adjoins significant tactical features or locations of national importance.

b. *Buffer Zone*. The Buffer Zone is the neutral space (or no-man's land) between ceasefire lines. It may contain residents and farmland which the Wider Peacekeeping force should monitor and protect. Otherwise access to buffer zones will be strictly controlled and normally only be allowed to the supervising authorities. The national civil authority's police may be allowed to enter the zone under the terms of a special agreement. The air space above a Buffer Zone will also be deemed as demilitarized and denied to aircraft of the parties concerned.

c. *Control Zones*. Control Zones are mutually agreed areas either side of the Buffer Zone, the forward limits of which will be the Ceasefire Lines. In those areas are set equal upper limits for numbers of personnel, tanks, artillery (by calibre), anti-aircraft weapons and missiles permitted in each area. Every situation will be unique, but in terms of distance from a Ceasefire Line will be based on whatever range makes attack into the opposing zone impossible. An example of a Control Zone might be as follows:

No military personnel within 5 kilometres.
No support weapons within 10 kilometres.
No armour, artillery or missiles within 30 kilometres.

The agreement and creation of Ceasefire Lines, Buffer Zones and Control Zones constitutes the geographic framework on which ceasefires are established and supervised.

17. **Delineation Factors**. The criteria used to determine critical terrain in war are not necessarily applicable to Wider Peacekeeping operations. A road, civic facility or centre of population in low ground may be more significant than fields of fire from high ground overlooking the area. Economic considerations should also be taken into account when determining a line so that, for example, a farmer is not denied access to water or a route to market for his animals.

18. **Delineation Procedures**. The following procedures should be used when delineating ceasefire lines, buffer zones and control zones:

a. If possible, obtain the agreement of all parties using a common large scale map.

b. Verify the line on the ground.

c. Provide an accurate and detailed description of the lines using agreed grid references.

d.   Survey and mark the lines on the ground using painted barrels, oil drums, stakes or wire. The markers should be secured in a way that makes them difficult to move.

e.   Agreed entry points to the zones should be clearly marked on the ground and the map

f.   A record of the lines, signed by all sides, should be given to the parties concerned with the original retained by the Wider Peacekeeping force. Alterations must be signed and promulgated in the same way.

g.   The use of air photography should be considered if practicable.

19.   *Area Ceasefires*. In many Wider Peacekeeping environments the opposing parties to a conflict may be inextricably mixed. In this situation a linear ceasefire line using a clear geographical delineation may not be possible. In the place of such ceasefires, areas might be agreed where ceasefires pertain. Area ceasefires of this nature will be difficult to enforce and will require close supervision.

20.   *Management of Ceasefires*. The effective management of a ceasefire will require numerous observers and liaison teams with independent, reliable and round-the-clock communications to both the Wider Peacekeeping authorities as well as the different parties to the conflict. Management measures should contain procedures for:

Investigation of alleged breaches of the ceasefire
Attribution of blame to transgressors
Retribution against offenders - ideally carried out by the parent factions of the guilty parties concerned.

Commanders should rehearse their management procedures and ensure that they remain in close contact with all the parties involved. A prompt, firm and fair reaction to breaches of ceasefire agreements is essential. Delayed and inappropriate reactions will prejudice the ceasefire's credibility and risk a rapid overall degeneration of the general security environment. It may be possible for the Wider Peacekeeping force to mount joint patrols with representatives from each of the factions involved. Such action will serve as a useful confidence-building measure.

STAGE 3 - WITHDRAWAL AND ASSEMBLY OF BELLIGERENTS

21.   Following a ceasefire, demobilization operations will require the coordinated disengagement and withdrawal of belligerents. This may be done by successively expanding or moving sectors of the buffer zone whilst keeping the Wider Peace-keeping force in between. The aim of this stage will be to move combatants away from the sustaining environment of their base areas and assemble them in secured locations where they can safely disarm. Opposing factions must be withdrawn simultaneously. This process is likely to require large numbers of troops and commanders will need to consider redeployment and reinforcement as a prepar-

atory measure. Because of shortage of manpower, the operation may have to be sequential, one small (but mutually balanced) area at a time. If supervised at theatre level, combatant elements, once moved to assembly locations, may be regrouped into cantonment areas, where they will remain long enough to allow assembly and disarmament to be completed theatre-wide. Once the cantonment areas are activated, parties will need to be accounted for and controlled. They will also require sustainment, including medical care. It may be appropriate to locate cantonment areas adjacent to civil infrastructure facilities so that the groups may be offered gainful employment in reconstructing and developing those facilities. Withdrawal and assembly of belligerent parties will also require the release and exchange of hostages, prisoners of war and bodies. Relocation and cantonment may also be required for vulnerable elements of the civil population although this will normally occur subsequently to the withdrawal and assembly of belligerents required by demobilization operations.

STAGE 4 - DISARMING OF BELLIGERENTS

22.   Disarming belligerents is likely to prove the most difficult and dangerous stage of demobilization. If done prematurely, the whole theatre of operations may be destabilized. Psychologically, parties to a conflict will only be prepared to disarm if they are confident that the preceding stages of the demobilization process have been securely carried out and that the resultant change in the security situation can be sustained in the long term. If the Wider Peacekeeper disarms local forces, he will be obliged to guarantee the security of the local population. Such a task is likely to prove demanding and manpower-intensive. Successful disarming will depend too on the combatant's trust of the Wider Peacekeeping force - both in terms of their impartiality as well as their state or region-wide credibility. The latter will depend on the public perception of the Wider Peacekeeping force's military capability and will to carry through the demobilization process, maintain the peace and punish transgressors. A perceived partiality or lack of resolve on the part of the supervising authorities will undermine the entire demobilization process, perhaps fatally. It may prove necessary to phase disarmament in a mutually balanced fashion. Besides collecting weapons from combatants, disarming will include the collection of war supplies from stockpiles and caches and the closure or control of munitions factories. The Wider Peacekeeping force may also have to interdict supply routes from neighbouring states. The custody and accurate accounting of weapons and war supplies will play a vital part in verifying the completion of the process. Industrial resources that could have a military application (for example petrol) may also need to be controlled.

STAGE 5 - DISPERSAL AND REHABILITATION OF BELLIGERENTS

23.   The final stage of demobilization operations is the dispersal and rehabilitation of belligerents. This stage is principally the responsibility of the civil authority and therefore leads into the next category of operations (Military Assistance). It is at this stage that military and civil responsibilities will overlap and careful judgement will be required to time the transition from one authority to the other. It may be that the trust built up between the parties to the conflict and the Wider Peacekeeping

force will argue for prolonging their involvement at this stage. At any rate, a transition of authority should only be made when it is judged to be safe. This stage of demobilization may be carried out in conjunction with the reconstitution and reform of the civil authority's police and defence forces which could well include former belligerents who might be re-armed, regrouped and placed under new authority. The planning and supervision of such reform might become the responsibility of a specified element of the Wider Peacekeeping force.

SECTION FOUR - MILITARY ASSISTANCE

INTRODUCTION

24.   Military Assistance refers to all forms of mandated assistance rendered by a Wider Peacekeeping force to a civil authority (ie a national or local government). In the absence of any effective government, military assistance may take the form of direct help given to civil communities. It covers a broad variety of possible tasks and may precede or follow a successfully conducted demobilization operation. In rendering military assistance, the Wider Peacekeeping force acts in support of the civil government according to the terms of a peace agreement or mandate. In Wider Peacekeeping operations, the principle of impartiality will still govern military actions. Force may be used, but not in a way that deliberately identifies particular factions as enemy. This means that the overall security situation must be relatively stable. Military assistance operations will therefore tend to occur in situations where the scale of violence and hostilities will have been reduced and military activities will have moved into a less dynamic phase allowing the reinstatement of a civil authority and the resumption of civil order. A broad consensual framework for operations will therefore exist. The commitment of military forces to assist an embattled government conduct counter insurgency operations would fall into the category of peace enforcement and is thus outside the scope of this manual.

LAW AND ORDER

25.   Military assistance operations will contribute to the overall aim of maintaining law and order - a responsibility that rests, in the first place, with the civil police. The maintenance of law and order constitutes the framework for all operational action and is essential to the successful establishment of civil authority. If law and order is failing, the aim of military assistance will be to restore the situation to the point where the police can once again effectively enforce the law. In this way, therefore, the Wider Peacekeeping force acts as the arm of the civil government and all its actions must be clearly seen to be in support of government policy. This will be achieved by coordinating civil and military actions and incorporating local security forces into military operations whenever possible.

PRINCIPLES AND TECHNIQUES OF MILITARY ASSISTANCE

26.   *Introduction*. The military assistance category of Wider Peacekeeping operations comprises a great variety of complex and sensitive tasks. It is therefore appropriate to develop and apply specifically to the military assistance scenario

particular principles and techniques which will reward observance. Those principles and techniques that apply more generally to Wider Peacekeeping as a whole are developed in a broader context in Chapters Four and Five.

27. ***Popular Support***. Military assistance operations will be impossible without a substantial degree of popular support. A principle purpose underlying every Wider Peacekeeping force activity will therefore be the acquisition and fostering of popular support. Effective civil affairs programmes ('hearts and minds' campaigns) will be key in this respect. The policy of the civil administration will be to establish such controls and protective measures as are necessary to gain public confidence and enhance society's support. Commanders should reinforce this aim at every opportunity and avoid using their troops in an unnecessarily provocative fashion or where they risk confrontation with the local population. Whenever possible the local populace should be encouraged to play an increasing role in their own protection. In addition to civil affairs programmes, commanders should also consider the potential for planning lower level community projects jointly with the local authorities so long as these are seen to be even-handed. Such projects should meet a genuine need, involve the overt participation of Wider Peacekeeping contingent and be directed at all sections of the community.

28. ***Minimum Force***. In a military assistance situation, the involvement and likely proximity of the local population makes the principle of minimum force particularly important to observe. The commander should never use more force than is necessary and reasonable to achieve his immediate military aim. All members of a Wider Peacekeeping force must be aware of the constraints which the law imposes on the use of force. Failure to observe the law will lead to a risk of prosecution, and possibly to civil proceedings for damages. Breaches of the law will also serve to alienate loyal and law-abiding members of the local population, and respect for the rule of law - the framework on which the entire military assistance campaign will be taking place - will be weakened if it appears that the law is being flouted by those whose task it is to uphold it.

29. ***Legality***. A Wider Peacekeeping force will usually be under obligation to observe strictly the relevant provisions of the national laws of the country in which it is operating - laws which may differ substantially from those pertaining to the United Kingdom. All military assistance operations should thus be conducted, and be seen to be conducted, within the law of the country where they are taking place. Commanders will be held responsible for their actions, and for those of their soldiers, who must not be exposed to the uncertainties of legal interpretation. This is properly a function of forward staff planning. However, if an unexpected change in circumstance has precluded such planning, commanders should initiate an urgent examination of the legal basis for military operations.

30. ***Coordination and Cooperation***. The successful conduct of military assistance operations depends on the effective coordination of civil and military effort. This coordination applies particularly to military and public information, security, planning, public safety, and operational direction. Such coordination is best achieved through centralized planning meetings in which the Wider Peacekeeping force and

civil administration are drawn together in order to formulate policy and implement it in a coordinated fashion at all levels. At the higher level, this coordination will be attained through the medium of a series of formally constituted committees. At lower levels centralized direction and control will be achieved through liaison, regular meetings and the use of joint operations rooms at each level of command. Centralized coordination will result in effective cooperation between the civil authority and the Wider Peacekeeping force. Such cooperation will be essential to emphasize the mutual confidence between them and to ensure that the conduct of operations is coherent and contributes directly to the achievement of government aims. Effective cooperation should be demonstrated at the earliest opportunity by the joint operation of Wider Peacekeeping forces and local security forces. To facilitate centralized direction and control, the boundaries of police and Wider Peacekeeping forces should coincide.

31. ***Concentration of Force.*** The principle of minimum necessary force does not imply 'minimum necessary troops'. A large element of a Wider Peacekeeping force speedily deployed at a critical location will demonstrate 'clout' and credibility and may enable a commander to use less force than he might otherwise have done - or even, by encouraging a peaceful resolution, to avoid using any force at all. Commanders must bear in mind, however, that a potentially peaceful situation could become hostile because of a provocative display of an over-large force.

32. ***Military Information.*** At each level, commanders should seek to establish a single, integrated military information organization. Ideally, the information and security elements of the civil administration and local security forces should be incorporated. The commander should task his military information organization with specific requirements to provide the timely information he needs.

33. ***Use of Local Security Forces.*** Local security forces in a military assistance situation are likely to be in need of support and encouragement, and they should be afforded, whenever possible, the opportunity of playing a useful and constructive part in operations. Indeed, the following local forces will have much to offer a Wider Peacekeeping force in terms of knowledge, expertise and resources:

   a. *Reserve Forces.* Local reserve, part-time or paramilitary forces should be employed on duties where their local knowledge and links with the community can be used to the full without exposing them to unreasonable pressures which could compromise their security.

   b. *Home Guards and Wardens.* Depending on the security situation it may be possible to establish locally recruited home guards or wardens to protect life and property in their own local areas. This would require them to be suitably armed and trained in order to perform static home guard duties, basic patrol tasks or act as wardens responsible for liaison with the people living in their sectors. They could prove extremely valuable in reporting information affecting local security to the authorities.

c.   *Coastguards, Frontier Service, Customs and Immigration.* The expertise and resources of coastguards, the frontier service, customs and immigration may be harnessed by Wider Peacekeeping forces in military assistance operations to provide surveillance and information as well as control the passage of both supplies and people. The communications of such organizations are usually good and their deployment comprehensive. Their assistance will represent little change from their peacetime roles. If possible within the bounds of security, commanders should ensure that they are liaising with and exploiting such organizations to the full.

Whenever possible, local security forces should operate with or alongside Wider Peacekeeping units. As areas are restored to order, local forces should assume control as part of the important transition process towards the civil authority regaining full responsibility.

34. **Public Information.** Through an effective public information programme commanders should seek to foster and maintain a good public image for their forces wherever they are deployed. This will be particularly important in a military assistance operation. The local populace will be kept in touch with government aims and intentions by means of public information activities. Through this means, it may be possible for the Wider Peacekeeping forces to explain the need for some of the restrictions being imposed and publicize other items of information that may prove helpful to both the public and military authorities. Hostile propaganda may be countered and the local population kept fully informed of government aims and policies. Every formation headquarters should have its own public information officer and staff with a press office open 24 hours a day. There should also be a press officer in each unit.

35. **Briefing.** In military assistance operations, commanders must ensure that they and their soldiers have received comprehensive briefings covering the background to the conflict and all aspects of the civil authority's activities and intentions. All Wider Peacekeeping personnel must be aware of the political aims of the government and of the measures devised to implement them. This will enable commanders to plan operations which are in accord with the civil administration's intentions and it will ensure that all ranks understand the reasons behind what they are doing and will react to unexpected situations appropriately.

MILITARY OPERATIONS

36. **Categories.** Military assistance tasks can be grouped in the following categories reflecting the purpose for which such tasks might be undertaken:

Supervision
Administration
Protection
Reaction
Control
Coordination

Each category of tasks is considered separately below:

SUPERVISION

37. There are a number of important supervisory tasks that a Wider Peacekeeping force might be required to carry out in a military assistance role:

    a. A transition of authority (possibly preceded by providing security for an election).

    b. Reforming local security forces including the provision of training, logistic and administrative support.

    c. The relocation and rehabilitation of refugees and other elements of a displaced population.

    d. The location, clearance and disposal of unexploded ordnance including mines (many of which may be unmarked) and improvised explosive devices. This task may prove an important contribution to the civil affairs programme and could include such things as the training of local nationals in mine clearance.

    e. Each of the above supervisory tasks will require specialist personnel and resources which will need to be tailored to the particular situation faced.

ADMINISTRATION

38. *Civil Administration*. When assistance to a civil authority is requested, it is likely that at least part of the government's administrative machinery will have broken down. The consequences of that administrative breakdown are likely eventually to affect the life of the entire community. When public services cease to function, rents and taxes fail to be collected, local authorities decline in effectiveness and subsequent disruptions can lead to rising unemployment and widespread dissatisfaction. In such circumstances a Wider Peacekeeping force may be invited to give additional assistance in the area of civil administration. This might range from liaison at one extreme to military government at the other.

39. *Public Utilities*. The supply of power, water, public transport, communications and health and hygiene services are an essential part of the fabric of life in a modern state and their disruption is consequently critical. A Wider Peacekeeping force may have much to offer in contributing to the maintenance of such essential services. Engineer resources will be particularly useful in lending practical assistance, offering advice or giving direction. Similarly, in remoter areas, special forces may be able to provide guidance and coordinate assistance to the civil administration. If committed to such a role, commanders should seek to retain as much of the civil labour force as possible, especially the skilled labour, although this may mean providing protection.

PROTECTION

40. ***Introduction***. Protective tasks include the safeguarding of individuals, communities and installations. Protective measures will tend to use up manpower. Commanders should therefore be mindful of the need to balance protective requirements against the need for more active operational measures.

41. ***Individuals***. Government officials, prominent citizens, members of the Wider Peacekeeping force or associated relief agencies and their families may be at risk in a military assistance scenario. The scale and extent of precautionary measures (such as the employment of close protection specialists) should be related to the threat, but contingency plans should be made for an increase in the threat. Commanders must make a thorough assessment of the problem and implement appropriate measures. Individuals may often be at their most vulnerable whilst travelling. Movement, by any means including road (in individual vehicles or by convoy) and rail should be protected by a combination of:

Precautionary Measures (including basic security safeguards)
Tactical Measures (for example escorts and picquets)
Contingency Measures (possibly including such things as airmobile reserve forces).

42. ***Protected Areas***. The aim of establishing protected areas is to create the conditions in a defined area within which a community will be able to respect and observe the law, and which will be protected from outside interference and attack. A protected area will be a region where, ultimately, the civil administration works and where the civil community is able to go about its business and live freely without fear. Having established such areas, the controlling authorities will aim to expand them in size and link them up. In Wider Peacekeeping operations, opposing factions may be inextricably mixed together within the area of operations, and establishing protected areas will therefore usually be complex undertakings and depend to a large degree on the cooperation and support of the resident population. The pursuit of civil affairs programmes and lower level community projects will therefore be critical to success in establishing protected areas. The development and participation of the civil administration is necessary if a protected area is going to have any chance of long-term success. Generally speaking, the establishment and maintenance of protected areas is fraught with difficulty since they will often cause friction, threaten the perceived impartiality of the Wider Peacekeeping force and demand large amounts of manpower.

43. ***Installations***. Responsibility for guarding all civil installations rest with the civil police. Military assistance may be required to supplement the police or take over from them if weapons or techniques are required which only the military can supply. Installations should be classified according to their status and commanders should view critically all requests to provide guards. Classification of installations and guard commitments should be regularly reviewed.

REACTION

44. The ability of a military force to react is essential to remaining balanced and regaining control over events. In all military assistance operations commanders should have reserves and contingency plans to assist the civil authority if required in dealing with outbreaks of violence including terrorism and riotous assemblies. The commander will normally be guided by these authorities, but he must make his own judgement as to what form of military assistance is appropriate, and he will remain accountable for his actions.

CONTROL

45. *Introduction*. In military assistance operations, commanders may be called upon to enforce collective control measures. Prohibitions and restrictions are always distasteful to the general public and the imposition of extra controls is likely to be particularly unpopular. Consequently such measures must be carefully planned. The need for them should be made clear, and they should be fairly and equitably applied. As with all military assistance operations, control measures which affect the civil population must be conducted within the law and no restriction should be placed on the movement or general freedom of civilians unless there is legal power or authority to do so.

46. *Aims*. The aims of applying controls will include:

    a. Improving the ability of the local security forces to enforce the law, thus increasing public confidence in government.

    b. Deterring violent or criminal activity.

    c. Restricting the potential for riotous assemblies.

    d. Limiting the illegal traffic of war supplies or contraband.

    e. Apprehending wanted persons.

    f. Detecting patterns of activity and gaining information.

47. *Application*. Control measures should be planned and directed on a joint police/ military basis with the fullest cooperation at every level. Ineffective controls will undermine public confidence in the security forces and measures should be applied firmly but with understanding. Whenever possible, explanations should be given to the public for actions taken. Controls should not be exercised for any longer than necessary. They may include road blocks, checkpoints, curfews, searches and patrols. Control measures are described in more detail in Chapter Five.

COORDINATION

48. If military assistance operations follow a conflict that has been particularly pro-longed, violent or widespread, there is likely to be a need for considerable support from relief agencies. A Wider Peacekeeping force may therefore be required to assist the civil authority in coordinating humanitarian relief efforts. This aspect is covered in more detail in the next section. Coordination tasks could include the investigation of war crimes and human rights abuses.

TIMING FORCE WITHDRAWAL

49. At a local level, commanders should continually review opportunities for returning responsibility to the civil authority. In general, the criterion for deciding whether to withdraw from a particular military assistance function will be whether or not that function can be protected and exercised by the civil authority without further assistance. Such decisions are sensitive and will require careful judgement. Too early a withdrawal may prove disastrous - but over-prolonged military commitment may prove nearly as harmful. Accordingly, the withdrawal of Wider Peacekeeping commitments within a military assistance operation should be flexible, taking account of the need to respond rapidly to political developments. There may even be a need to recommit military forces. In general, commanders should therefore consider withdrawal from particular military commitments in three possible ways:

   a. Rapidly (if the prospect of success seems assured).

   b. Gradually (in phases which can be slowed down or speeded up). Such phases may relate to functions or geographical regions.

   c. Partially (by changing the role of the Wider Peacekeeping force from direct to indirect assistance).

SECTION FIVE - HUMANITARIAN RELIEF

INTRODUCTION

50. *Scope*. Humanitarian aid, particularly in the relatively orderly conditions of negotiated ceasefires, was generally part and parcel of Cold War peacekeeping operations. This section does not cover routine humanitarian activities such as economic assistance and intermediary duties. Instead it covers the deeper commitment that now exists post Cold War to giving humanitarian relief to those in drastic conditions, often in situations of chaos. Humanitarian relief operations are likely to become a focus for attention within the context of a Wider Peacekeeping scenario and may exert a profound influence on the overall course of events. In certain circumstances, but making every effort not to compromise the neutrality of the relief agencies, they may also be used as a tool by the commander to reward the compliance of belligerent factions.

51. **Legal Basis**. In a situation of internal conflict there are certain provisions of international law that apply to the granting of humanitarian relief. For example, Article 3 of each of the four Geneva Conventions of 1949 relating to the Protection of War Victims lays down certain minimum humanitarian standards which are to be adopted in cases of 'armed conflict not of an international character' occurring in the territory of a party to the Conventions.

52. **Context**. Humanitarian relief operations may be carried out in conjunction with other Wider Peacekeeping tasks or completely independently. In most humanitarian relief situations it is likely that a broad variety of international civil agencies will be involved including the UN, and government, non-government and private voluntary organizations. Examples of such agencies include the United Nations Department of Humanitarian Affairs (UNDHA), the United Nations High Commissioner for Refugees (UNHCR), the International Committee of the Red Cross and Red Crescent (ICRC), Medecins Sans Frontieres (MSF) and the International Rescue Committee (IRC) - any of which might constitute the overall coordinating authority. Humanitarian relief operations could therefore occur under different guidance, authority and conditions. They might be conducted locally or state-wide and possibly be denied the cooperation of the local authorities. The Wider Peacekeeping force should exercise caution in lending direct support to non-accredited aid agencies since they may be involved in illegal activities (such as the movement of weapons) and could thus, by association, prejudice the contingent's legitimacy.

TARGETS OF HUMANITARIAN RELIEF

53. **Displaced Persons and Refugees**. The migration of displaced persons (those forced to leave their homes) and refugees (those forced to leave their countries) is a common feature of most Wider Peacekeeping situations. The departure or removal of such people from their native supporting environments is likely to put them in need of humanitarian relief. The numbers of those requiring help can range from small parties of individuals to entire ethnic groups.

54. **Residents**. Humanitarian relief may also be required for resident communities which are at risk from the activities of warring parties, famine, drought or ecological disasters, the latter categories often brought about by conflict.

PHASES OF HUMANITARIAN RELIEF OPERATIONS

55. Wider Peacekeeping forces are likely to become involved in two particular phases of humanitarian relief operations:

   a. *Emergency Phase*. The aim of the emergency phase is to save lives. It will therefore entail the provision of vital services and the distribution of the basic requirements for survival, namely food, water, fuel, shelter and medical care. Emphasis will be on the assembly and rescue of victims and, if necessary, transporting them away from a life-threatening environment. Emergency medical care will be crucial component of this phase.

b.   *Administration Phase*. When the targets of humanitarian relief are no longer in immediate danger, the emphasis of the operation will shift to continuing the administration of those rescued and setting in hand arrangements for their subsequent rehabilitation and the reconstruction of public services.

PRINCIPLES OF HUMANITARIAN RELIEF OPERATIONS

56.   **Liaison and Coordination**. NGOs and community leaders will always have much to offer in terms of influence, information and linguistic skills. Commanders should therefore always seek to liaise with and gain the support of NGOs and community leaders to enlist their cooperation and improve the coordination of relief activity. To this end, they should be involved, as much as possible, in the planning and supervision of activities. If feasible, they should be taken on reconnaissance trips and also included in such things as briefings, orders and advance parties.

57.   **Security**. Whenever possible, commanders should place priority on demobilizing and securing the area within which humanitarian operations are to be mounted. The benefit of humanitarian operations will be minimized if they are not conducted within an effective security framework. There will be little long-term utility, for example, in providing humanitarian relief to communities who are in imminent danger of extermination from warring factions. A secure environment also provides better protection for humanitarian convoys than isolated escorts.

58.   **Timeliness**. Timeliness is critical factor to the success of humanitarian relief operations. Information, intelligence, reconnaissance, mobility, speed of reaction and effective planning and staff work will all contribute to humanitarian operations being mounted in a timely fashion.

59.   **Priorities**. The planning and execution of humanitarian relief operations should always reflect a careful prioritization of the targets and their needs. This prioritization will be reflected in the composition, equipment and supplies of relief teams. The movement of relief personnel and supplies to the target area should also be prioritized to meet the most urgent needs first.

60.   **Unity of Effort**. Whenever possible, commanders should encourage the establishment of coordinating mechanisms in which all appropriate agencies are represented. The mechanisms should be supported by widespread liaison and reliable communications.

MILITARY TASKS

61.   Military tasks pertaining to humanitarian relief are likely to fall into the following categories:

a.   Protection of delivery and relief workers (against conflicting parties to a conflict or criminal elements).

b. Establishment, support and protection of regional safe havens and protected areas.

c. Administrative tasks, including the coordination of relief agencies and distribution of supplies. Special forces are often particularly suited to this task.

d. Engineer support, including road construction and maintenance, bridging and infrastructure engineering.

e. Sustainment, including transportation, supply, maintenance and medical support.

f. Many of the above tasks will overlap with those in the military assistance categories.

SECTION SIX - GUARANTEE AND DENIAL OF MOVEMENT

62. Chapter Two described the guarantee and denial of movement as those operations mandated to guarantee or deny movement by air, land, or sea in particular areas and over certain routes. At the tactical level, military tasks associated with such operations might include the guarding or denying of passage on overland routes - perhaps to relieve a besieged community or to contain the activities of belligerent parties, and the enforcement of no-fly zones to prevent the harassment of an unprotected population. Guarantee and denial measures may overlap with conflict prevention measures, including preventive deployment. Commanders may employ a wide range of forces to undertake such missions, including infantry, armour, engineer, aviation and air defence assets. The effective use of such resources may require the coordinated employment of electronic emissions, as well as access to high-level military information assessments. Operations to guarantee and deny movement will also usually involve the coordinated commitment of theatre-level assets. The operations are generally sensitive, carrying as they do the risk of sudden escalation and the possible prejudicing of impartiality. Their management and subsequent development may hinge on the interpretation of Rules of Engagement. Guarantee and denial of movement operations are therefore normally controlled at the operational or strategic level and will not be considered in further detail here.

CHAPTER FOUR

PRINCIPLES

"Still in thy right hand carry gentle peace,
To silence envious tongues."

William Shakespeare

SECTION ONE - INTRODUCTION

1. ***Requirement***. The normal principles of war are predicated on the identification of an enemy. The impartial status of those undertaking Wider Peacekeeping operations, however, means that there are no enemy forces - only parties to the conflict amongst whom the Wider Peacekeeper plays a supervisory rôle. Not all the standard principles of war are therefore appropriate for direct application to Wider Peacekeeping operations. This is not to suggest that all such principles should be abandoned or that Wider Peacekeeping will not require the highest professional military standards. Indeed, the risk of uncontrolled transition to a peace enforcement scenario may often be present and all categories of Wider Peacekeeping tasks are likely to require the employment of soundly-trained and well-motivated soldiers. Existing procedures and structures of professional forces will therefore probably prove appropriate to many of the situations faced. However, as Chapter Two has explained, a different conceptual approach is required for the supervisory third party nature of Wider Peacekeeping. This means that particular principles must be identified to guide the conduct of such operations.

> **CONTENTS**
>
> INTRODUCTION
>   Requirement
>   Emphasis
>   Principles
>
> CONSENT PRINCIPLES
>   Impartiality
>   Minimum Force
>   Legitimacy
>   Credibility
>   Mutual Respect
>   Transparency
>
> MANAGEMENT PRINCIPLES
>   Coherence
>   Coordination and Liaison
>   Flexibility
>   Security
>   Concentration of Force
>   Freedom of Movement

2. ***Emphasis***. Wider Peacekeeping depends upon local support and cooperation for success. It is a conflict resolution, not termination, activity where ends are achieved by persuasion rather than the use of force. Coercion, even if practicable in the short term, will foster resentment and hostility, engendering risk and instability which will ultimately prove counter-productive. The promotion and sustaining of consent is therefore key to success and will represent the commander's primary concern. This concern should guide the planning and conduct of all operations.

3. ***Principles***. This chapter therefore identifies and seeks to explain general and enduring principles that should be applied to Wider Peacekeeping operations. The principles are divided into two categories - consent and management.

CONSENT PRINCIPLES	MANAGEMENT PRINCIPLES
Impartiality	Coherence
Minimum Force	Coordination and Liaison
Legitimacy	Flexibility
Credibility	Security
Mutual Respect	Concentration of Force
Transparency	Freedom of Movement

The understanding and application by commanders of the foregoing Wider Peacekeeping principles will be foundational to success. Both categories should be carefully applied to operational activity at all stages. However, particular emphasis should be laid on those consent principles that encourage and develop local support and cooperation. Despite their intangibility, it is through the application of such principles that perceptions will be changed and conflict ultimately resolved.

SECTION TWO - CONSENT PRINCIPLES

IMPARTIALITY

4. ***A Vital Characteristic***. As Chapter Two made clear, impartiality with respect to the belligerents is a prime doctrinal interpretation of the consent criterion. Without impartiality, there can be no prospect of preserving the confidence and cooperation of conflicting factions. Impartiality is thus a vital characteristic of those undertaking Wider Peacekeeping operations. The notion of impartiality is as much a matter of perception as of practice. It is not enough for wider peacekeepers to act impartially - they must be seen to be acting impartially. Just as consent is likely to be incomplete, so impartiality is likely to prove inexact and fragmentary in practice. Indeed, impartiality will be constantly challenged and threatened in most Wider Peacekeeping scenarios. The more complex the situation, the more difficult it will be for the peacekeeper to preserve his impartial status and retain the confidence of all parties. The more active the rôle of the peacekeeper, the more likely this is to be true. Separate factions may be expected continually to seek to advance their own interests through the offices of the Wider Peacekeeper and it will often suit individual belligerent parties to portray the peacekeeping force as favouring their opponents. Nevertheless, impartiality remains the vital characteristic of operational conduct and must be protected at all costs.

5. ***Consequences of Loss of Impartiality***. The loss, perceived or real, of impartiality may have very serious consequences. At best, loss of impartiality is likely to result in the displacement of any trust and confidence that a Wider Peacekeeping force might have with local factions, thus limiting the options open to the force in resolving the conflict. At worst, the loss of impartiality could trigger an uncontrolled escalation to a peace enforcement scenario leading to widespread and unre-

strained violence, heavy civilian and military casualties and the failure of the mission.

6. ***Preservation of Impartiality***. Commanders should therefore aim to preserve and demonstrate impartiality whenever possible. All dealings by UN troops, whether operational, administrative or social should be conducted without favour to any particular party or any single point of view. Even such actions as offering lifts may be misinterpreted, innocently or deliberately, by onlookers. Balance should be sought in all activities. Threats to impartiality will thrive on ignorance and misunderstanding. Consequently, commanders should make repeated efforts at the earliest opportunity to explain clearly the rôle of their forces and to develop the best possible relations with all elements of the local communities. Regular contacts and conference opportunities will need to be maintained with all parties to the conflict. An active and imaginative public and community information campaign will prove an essential tool for such tasks.

7. ***A Critical Determinant***. Commanders should use the impartiality criterion as a critical determinant of all planning and conduct including, for example, the use of force. Chapter Two has already made clear that impartiality does not equate to the non-use of force - force might be used against aggressors irrespective of their parent factions in the protection of a Wider Peacekeeping mandate. However, the use of force that sought deliberately to favour or penalize a particular party to the conflict would evidently compromise impartiality, thus seriously destabilizing a Wider Peacekeeping operation.

MINIMUM FORCE

8. ***Introduction***. 'Minimum force' describes the body of principles governing the use of force. These principles will assist the commander in decision-making concerning the use of force. Rules Of Engagement (ROE), international, domestic and host nation law are authoritative and establish limits on the use of force. However, such limits usually offer little guidance on how to respond to particular tactical situations. Minimum force principles must therefore be considered and applied on a case-by-case basis.

9. ***Significance and Scope***. The way in which force is used will be a critical determinant of the course that a Wider Peacekeeping operation takes. Solutions that are imposed without the consent of the belligerents are, by their very nature, liable to become sources of future resentment and hostility which may inhibit control and become manifest in outbreaks of further violence and prolongation of the conflict. The long term effects of force may prove substantially different from the short term ones - a tactical success resulting from the use of force may lead to a long term strategic failure. This is because the use of force in a Wider Peacekeeping environment is likely to have profound repercussions that go beyond the demands of the immediate tactical situation. Many aspects of the overall operation are likely to be affected. The use of force tends in the long term to attract a response in kind and its use may heighten tension, polarize opinion, foreclose negotiating opportunities, prejudice the perceived impartiality of the

Wider Peacekeeping contingent, and escalate the overall level of violence. Its use may embroil a peacekeeping force in a harmful long-term conflict that is irrelevant to the campaign aim. Collateral damage may also set back any developing civil affairs programme and adversely affect the overall attitude of the indigenous population to the Wider Peacekeeping contingent. The use of force therefore carries disproportionate risk of which commanders at all levels must take careful account, and decisions concerning its application are likely to prove the most critical that a commander will take. The use of force is a complex topic with many facets. It represents a crucial aspect of Wider Peacekeeping operations and merits the closest attention of all military personnel. The conceptual approach to the use of force described in Chapter Two should be understood by all commanders.

10.   **Approach**. The Wider Peacekeeper has many factors to take into account when reaching a decision on the use of force. He should always perform a mission analysis which transcends the short term requirements of the tactical situation and takes into account the long term campaign aims. To preserve the consensual framework so vital to success in Wider Peacekeeping operations, commanders should seek to defuse situations, de-escalate rather than inflame tensions and lend preference to actions that in the long term move the situation downwards through the spectrum of violence. There should be a reluctance rather than predisposition to the use of force, but with due regard to credibility. Generally speaking, in a Wider Peacekeeping operation, commanders should regard its use as a last resort.

11.   **Alternatives**. Alternatives to the use of force include the following:

   a.   *Deterrence*. The requirement to use force may be avoided through the skilful use of deterrent measures such as interposition or deployment in strength. The presence of sufficient numbers of forces at the scene of a potential incident will tend to diminish the confidence of a would-be aggressor and allow the commander on the spot a wider spectrum of options to counter an incident. An insufficient force level at the scene of a crisis is more likely to require resort to a harmful use of force. Good planning and rehearsals will characterise anticipatory deterrent measures.

   b.   *Threats*. An implicit (ie unspecified) threat is no different from deterrence. However, consideration may occasionally be given to the use of explicit threats. Such threats must be credible, thus committing a commander to the possible use of force. A commander should therefore never make threats that he is unsure of being able to carry out. Threats should not go beyond the limit of actions that might destabilize a peacekeeping scenario by rupturing consent at the operational level. As such they should be the penultimate resort before the use of force. If made, threats should be strictly impartial and have at least the implicit prior consent of belligerent leaders and interested parties.

   c.   *Negotiation and Mediation*. Negotiation and mediation may be used to reconcile differences among belligerents both to each other and the Wider Peacekeeping force. In many societies, self-esteem and group honour are of great importance and simple face-saving measures to preserve a party's dignity may serve to relax tension and defuse a crisis.

d. *Control Measures*. Control measures such as pre-planned or improvised roadblocks, cordons, curfews, access control and checkpoints may be employed to avoid the use of force. For example vehicles might be used to block thoroughfares or remove unauthorized persons from sensitive locations. Sniping may be constrained by limiting the movement of weapons or by denying access to vantage points. Similarly, the potential for riots may be mitigated by restricting the ability of crowds to assemble.

e. *Rewards and Penalties*. Force is not the only means of compulsion. Rewards and penalties can often be used to encourage cooperation. When military forces control the distribution of basic resources, such resources can be withheld or granted to direct and shape local behaviour and cooperation. However, such action must be carefully judged in order not to compromise the impartial image of the contingent in the eyes of the local population.

f. *Protection*. Effective protection, for example armoured personnel carriers, will reduce the opportunities open to would-be aggressors to mount attacks on Wider Peacekeeping contingents and will deflate the confidence of belligerent parties. In the event of being attacked, effective protection will obviate the necessity of an early resort by peacekeeping forces to lethal responsive measures. In a crisis, effective protection will allow the considered application of a wider range of non-lethal options.

g. *Warning*. Parties to a conflict should be left in no doubt about the circumstances under which a Wider Peacekeeping contingent might be obliged to use force. If appropriate, warning procedures for each circumstance should be provided to the belligerents and they should be given specific warnings if their continuing activities are likely to incur a use of force.

h. *Non-Lethal Use of Force*. Force itself need not be lethal. When authorized, riot control agents and other measures such as the use of batons, may preclude the need to resort to more deadly measures. Commanders should therefore develop and practice the capabilities for measured non-lethal responses to potential crises.

A timely response is usually essential in containing potential crises and limiting escalation. Alternatives to the use of force should therefore be carried out on the spot and at the lowest level possible. Pre-planning, anticipatory briefing and rehearsal are essential preparatory measures.

12. **Rules of Engagement (ROE)**. ROE are directives that delineate the circumstances and limitations under which force may be used. ROE will reflect legal, political and diplomatic constraints and will have been developed at the highest level outside the theatre. In Wider Peacekeeping situations, ROE will always authorize the self-defence of those conducting operations. They may also offer extended

powers to use force in defence of mandated activities, for example the delivery of humanitarian aid. However, ROE will seldom anticipate every situation and commanders and leaders at all levels must interpret them intelligently in the light of long-term campaign aims. ROE should never inhibit a commander's responsibility to take all necessary and appropriate action to protect his force.

13. **Requesting Changes to ROE**. Commanders at all levels may request changes to ROE. The requirement to change the ROE may result from local tactical emergencies. Situations requiring an immediate change to ROE might include the intervention of combat forces from a hostile nation or attacks by sophisticated weapon systems including nuclear, biological, or chemical devices.

14. **Guidelines**. If force has to be used, it should be controlled by the following principles:

   a. *Impartiality*. Impartiality is a crucial determinant of the methods by which force might be employed. As a guideline it should therefore be uppermost in the minds of commanders. The abandonment of impartiality equates to the abandonment of the Wider Peacekeeping contingent's third party supervisory rôle. In using force in such a way, the contingent would be seen to be taking sides and joining the conflict. The damage to its perceived legitimacy would prejudice the contingent's security as well as its ability to supervise belligerent activities. Force should therefore always be used impartially - that is to say not applied in ways that might be seen as deliberately favouring or penalizing particular factions.

   b. *Minimum Necessary Force*. Minimum necessary force is defined as the measured application of violence or coercion, sufficient only to achieve a specific end, demonstrably reasonable, proportionate and appropriate; and confined in effect to the specific and legitimate target intended. Only the appropriate amount of force proportional to the particular situation should be used. The degree of force used must be no greater than that reasonably necessary under the circumstances. Non-lethal force would normally be appropriate to control disturbances, uphold law and order, and to apprehend or detain criminals. Controlling force in this way will demand restraint, discipline and control. Unnecessary collateral damage must be avoided at all costs. Reprisals and the pre-emptive (ie first use) of force are inappropriate to Wider Peacekeeping operations.

   c. *Observe Legal Limits*. ROE, international, domestic and host nation law establish authoritative limits on the ways and means in which force may be used. Those limits should not be transgressed.

   d. *Firmness*. The use of force should be accompanied at every stage by a display of firmness and determination. If a Wider Peacekeeping unit is seen to lack confidence, it may be further challenged, resulting in an unnecessarily high level of response

e.   *Warning.* If possible, the use of force should be preceded by clear warnings

f.   *Escape Route.* Before using force, a peacekeeping unit must ensure that belligerents can disperse or withdraw safely from the incident. Lethal force should not be used against belligerents who are in a position from which they cannot escape

g.   *Defensive Locations.* In anticipation of the consequences of using force, defensive locations should be reconnoitred, prepared for occupation and protected. If appropriate, such locations should include shelters to protect troops from shell, mortar and rocket fire. Their occupation must be rehearsed.

LEGITIMACY

15. ***Legality and Propriety.*** Legitimacy derives from the perception that the Wider Peacekeeping mission, as well as its execution of the mission, is just. The higher the degree of legitimacy ascribed to the Wider Peacekeeping force by the international community and the parties to the conflict, the greater is the likelihood of success. It is therefore essential that military forces act, and are seen to act within the domestic, national, international and military law, as well as within the UN Mandate and the Status Of Forces Agreement. Perceived failure to do so could strip the force of its legitimacy, authority and, ultimately, its operational effectiveness. Legitimacy will also encourage the wider participation of the international community and non-governmental organizations. Commanders must beware of doing anything that might prejudice the perceived legitimacy of their forces. Inappropriate conduct off duty or the slightest evidence of corrupt practices at any level will damage the overall legitimacy of the contingent. The highest standards of conduct and integrity must be observed by all personnel. Commanders must be prepared to take severe disciplinary action against those who violate such standards.

CREDIBILITY

16. ***Components.*** Wider Peacekeeping operations demand the commitment of a credible force. Such credibility will depend on the force's perceived capability to carry out particular tasks. Only then will those concerned (including the belligerents) have confidence in the force's activities. Credibility is a key psychological element of success and, at the tactical level, will derive from three elements:

Resources

Execution

Concept of operations

Adequate resources must be effectively employed in pursuing a realistic concept of operations. It is a question of striking a balance between being strong enough to pursue the concept without being over provocative.

17. **Practice**. Credibility should be high on the commander's list of considerations and will devolve from demonstrations of a manifest capability backed up by a will to use it. Gross violations of the UN mandate by belligerents should be answered quickly and correctly. The first few hours of a ceasefire, for example, are the most important to enforce. All personnel of a Wider Peacekeeping force must bolster their force's credibility by a consistent, disciplined, thorough and effective performance of their duties. At the tactical level, credibility will demand balanced forces that can escalate or de-escalate their activities as required.

MUTUAL RESPECT

18. **External**. The Wider Peacekeeping environment is likely to create friction between the recognized parties to a conflict and the Wider Peacekeeping force. Notwithstanding such friction, the force should always hold the respect of the belligerent factions. If that respect has been lost, action should be taken as a matter of priority to restore it. Such respect should be mutual and, whilst a Wider Peacekeeping force will enjoy certain immunities, its members must respect the host country's laws, language, religion, culture and social customs and show patience and respect for the problems and negotiating positions of the belligerents wherever possible. Gratuitous offence to local cultures are likely to prove seriously counterproductive and should be avoided at all costs. Mutual respect, if fostered, will contribute to the development of local trust and confidence so essential to the overall consensual framework of a Wider Peacekeeping operation.

19. **Internal**. This principle also applies to relationships within a multinational Wider Peacekeeping force where mutual respect should be cultivated between the various nationalities represented. The multinational nature of forces conducting Wider Peacekeeping operations allows no place for national prejudices and chauvinism. Lack of sensitivities in this area may create profound damage to long-term prospects of success.

TRANSPARENCY

20. It is important that a Wider Peacekeeping force's actions should not be misinterpreted by the parties to the conflict or the local populace. Such misunderstandings may prove dangerous in times of tension. A force's activities should therefore be manifestly 'above-board' and not be vulnerable to accusations of pursuing an illicit hidden agenda. Consistent with the prevailing requirements for operational security, therefore, the parties to a conflict in a Wider Peacekeeping environment should be made as fully aware as possible of the motive, mission and intentions of the UN force. A failure to communicate this will foster suspicion and may prevent the development of confidence and trust, thus prejudicing prospects for future conciliation and cooperation. Transparency is therefore a highly desirable characteristic of Wider Peacekeeping operations and should be promoted whenever possible. It will require active management.

SECTION THREE - MANAGEMENT PRINCIPLES

COHERENCE

21. ***Objectives***. The UN mandate will determine the overall aim of the Wider Peacekeeping force. At the tactical level this aim must be translated into clearly defined, coherent and achievable objectives towards which all military activity is directed so that unity of effort is achieved. These objectives must be fully understood and consistently pursued by all members of the Wider Peacekeeping force at every level. It is through the common pursuit of such objectives that coherence will be achieved. Provided the security of the force is not prejudiced, parties to the conflict should be fully appraised of these objectives and, if possible, be afforded opportunities of contributing to their achievement.

22. ***Limitations***. When formulating the objectives, tactical commanders must take full account of the limitations imposed by the Mandate, Status of Forces Agreement, Rules of Engagement and other factors. However, submission to such limitations should not inhibit the fullest consideration and exploitation of whatever residual scope there might be for imaginative military operations which consistently pursue realistic objectives.

COORDINATION AND LIAISON

23. ***Coordination***. As well as being multinational, Wider Peacekeeping operations are likely to involve a wide range of organizations including civil powers, UN relief agencies and non-governmental organizations. Privately-sponsored individuals may also be taking part in activities such as humanitarian relief. Many of these agencies and individuals are highly sensitive to perceived infringements to their independence and commanders must appreciate that their coordination can only be by consent, not direction. Commanders must also appreciate that even at the lowest tactical level their own actions may be but one element of a variety of diplomatic and humanitarian activities over which they have no direct control. Nevertheless the timely and effective coordination of these agencies is likely to prove essential to the successful execution of the campaign plan at the tactical level. Commanders should therefore seek to establish coordination mechanisms that take account of these sensitivities yet still impart coherence to all elements of activity in their operational area. As well as military operations, the coordination mechanisms should embrace political, diplomatic, civil, administrative, legal and humanitarian agents including the press and other internationally-sponsored military and civil contingents in the area, civil police, administrative representatives, and ongoing negotiations with the parties to the conflict.

24. ***Liaison***. Coordination mechanisms should be supported by extensive liaison with all involved parties and communities upwards, downwards and sideways. The ability to deploy large numbers of liaison officers with their own transport and communications will prove invaluable to the commander, both for information and coordination purposes. The more complex the environment, the larger will be the number of liaison officers required and commanders will usually want more liaison

officers than they have. Liaison officer skills should match those of the organization with whom they are to liaise (eg engineer to engineer, military police to police and so on) since there will be an obvious common interest between the parties and a reasonably similar modus operandi. To facilitate liaison, commanders should seek to co-locate their command posts with leading UN representatives in the area. Reliable communications are vital to coordination and liaison and should be backed up by alternative systems. The demands of liaison may slow the planning and execution of operations but will prove a critical element of success. Liaison techniques are described in Chapter Five.

FLEXIBILITY

25. Wider Peacekeeping operations cover a wide range of tasks, each of which has the potential for rapid transit up and down the intensity spectrum. This characteristic renders flexibility a key attribute for those undertaking such operations. The Wider Peacekeeping force should be able to adapt and move from one activity to another as required - at short notice and with the minimum of outside assistance. Wider Peacekeeping teams should therefore, whenever possible, be structured so as to be balanced and independent in terms of skills, capabilities, equipment, self-defence and logistics. Arrangements to facilitate the speedy availability of reserves should also be considered. Skilful anticipation by commanders may often serve to pre-empt crises. At any rate, commanders must rehearse contingency plans for transitions in intensity and possible requirements to extract their forces or conduct relief in place.

SECURITY

26. In situations of chaos, the impartial and legitimate status of Wider Peacekeeping contingents may not afford them the protection they deserve, either as groups or individuals. Self-defence is an intrinsic right of UN-mandated activity and commanders should ensure that adequate arrangements exist at all times for the protection of their forces. Requirements for protection could also extend to civil agencies and non-governmental organizations. Whenever possible, Wider Peacekeeping commanders should seek to establish a viable security framework within which operations are mounted. In humanitarian operations for example, a secure route and protected destination is a better guarantee of safety than convoy escorts, although both will normally be required. Locally employed civilians must be carefully vetted before they are allowed access to military facilities. Their security status should be regularly reviewed.

CONCENTRATION OF FORCE

27. A maximum presence of forces on the ground will often be desirable for Wider Peacekeeping operations, both for deterrence, credibility and information-gathering purposes and for domination, albeit discreetly, of the general environment. The deployment plans and daily routine of a Wider Peacekeeping force should therefore take this factor into account. The need to maintain a visible and confident presence, however, should be balanced against the possibility of such deployments

being perceived as gratuitously provocative gestures. The safety of troops and availability of reserves will also be pertinent considerations. Commanders should develop the mobility required to concentrate their forces quickly at the scenes of potential incidents.

FREEDOM OF MOVEMENT

28. Freedom of movement is essential to Wider Peacekeeping contingents. A force which cannot move to and within its area of operation to conduct its tasks will fail to accomplish its mission. The force's privileges and rights relating to movement will be outlined in the Mandate and Status Of Forces Agreement. The fundamental facility of free movement should be protected and exploited by tactical commanders at every opportunity. Routes, for example, should be kept open even when not in use.

CHAPTER FIVE

OPERATIONAL TECHNIQUES

"Though this be madness, yet there is method in 't."
William Shakespeare

SECTION ONE - INTRODUCTION

1. ***Overview***. A Wider Peacekeeping force will normally carry out the operational tasks described in Chapter Three using a combination of the techniques described below. Like Chapter Four's principles, the techniques fall into two categories - consent and management:

    CONSENT TECHNIQUES
    Negotiation and Mediation
    Liaison
    Civil Affairs
    Community Information
    Public Information
    Community Relations

    MANAGEMENT TECHNIQUES

    Military Information
    Observation and Monitoring
    Interposition
    Supervision
    Control Measures
    Patrolling

CONTENTS

INTRODUCTION

CONSENT TECHNIQUES:

Negotiation and Mediation
Liaison
Civil Affairs
Community Information
Public Information
Community Relations

MANAGEMENT TECHNIQUES:

Military Information
Observation and Monitoring
Interposition
Supervision
Control Measures
Patrolling

The consent techniques address attitudes and perceptions directly and are therefore of critical utility in preserving and developing consent in order to facilitate the ultimate resolution of the conflict. The management techniques afford physical control of the operational environment. In so doing they create the opportunities for the consent techniques to be employed.

2. ***Force Structures***. Force structures required to employ these techniques will vary. In some instances unarmed or lightly armed personnel in small groups will suffice. In the case of techniques like interposition, larger groups of armed soldiers may be required with armoured protection, indirect fire assets and on-call reinforcements. Such groups may well be of multinational composition or made up by troops from a single nation.

3. ***Involvement of Belligerent Parties***. The surest way of consolidating a consensual framework will be by engendering the active involvement of belligerent parties in the Wider Peacekeeping process. If parties to a conflict can be delegated responsibilities which confer vested interests in the successful outcome of a Wider Peacekeeping operation - if they can, in effect, be made shareholders in the peace process, then their willingness to cooperate will be greatly increased. Whenever possible, therefore, parties to the conflict should be given opportunities to cooperate together in providing specific services that contribute to the resolution of the conflict - for example joint patrols, checkpoints and the protection of humanitarian aid. Such opportunities should be linked to incentives and reinforced with appropriate rewards and penalties. Involvement in tasks in this way is not without risk, however, and will require close supervision by elements of the Wider Peacekeeping force. The perceived impartiality of the Wider Peacekeeping contingent must not be set at risk. Nevertheless, commanders should continually review such means of applying operational techniques and reinforcing consent.

SECTION TWO - CONSENT TECHNIQUES

NEGOTIATION AND MEDIATION

4. ***Description***. The terms may be described as follows:

    a. **Negotiation** refers to direct dialogue between parties. If negotiating itself, the Wider Peacekeeping force will be playing an active rôle to gain particular ends whilst protecting its own interests. Such negotiations might take place to secure the safe passage of humanitarian relief supplies.

    b. **Mediation** describes the activities of a go-between connecting parties to a dispute. In this rôle the Wider Peacekeeper has no position of his own to guard - he acts as the means whereby opposing parties communicate with each other and he encourages them to identify and reach mutually agreed solutions.

    c. **Conciliation** describes the reconciling effect wrought on opposing parties to a conflict by agreements resulting from successful negotiation and mediation.

    The ultimate aim of negotiation and mediation is to reach agreements to which all parties have freely concurred. Such agreements will normally represent compromises between the aims of the participants.

5. ***Significance***. Chapter Two has highlighted the key significance of promoting and sustaining consent in Wider Peacekeeping operations. Article 33 of Chapter VI of the UN Charter emphasizes the importance of negotiation, enquiry, mediation and conciliation as the priority means of settling disputes. By negotiation and mediation, positive relationships between the factions and the Wider Peacekeeping force will be formed, enabling agreements to be reached and promoting the process of conciliation. Objective and effective negotiations created, controlled and fostered at every level by the Wider Peacekeeping force will develop a climate of mutual

respect and cooperation. The techniques of negotiation and mediation are therefore likely to prove the primary and most potent means of developing peaceful, agreeable and lasting solutions to conflict in all aspects of a Wider Peacekeeping operation.

6. ***Requirement***. Negotiation and mediation will be required at all stages of a Wider Peacekeeping operation and will need to be exercised at every level. Consequently all participants will be involved - from senior commanders meeting with faction leaders, to individual soldiers at isolated observation points who might find themselves arbitrating a dispute. Confrontations may be sudden and unexpected, and negotiation and mediation could be required immediately without preparation in situations where life and limb may be at stake.

7. ***Complexity***. Negotiating sessions are likely to be characterized at all levels by the representation of numerous interested parties. Some will be directly involved, others will have peripheral interests. The relationship between the representatives will be complex and often competitive. All representatives are likely to play a rôle in the outcome of the negotiations. Participants may represent the broadest and most complicated range of interests, perceptions, bargaining tools and cultural approaches - each element of which will interact and possibly conflict with the others present. The interplay of personalities will contribute significantly to the course and outcome of the negotiations.

8. ***Conduct of Negotiations and Mediation.*** There are three stages in the process of negotiation and mediation. They are: preparation, conduct and follow-up. All require extensive consideration, research and care. These are described below.

9. ***Preparation***. First; a clear aim should be defined; the Wider Peacekeeper should seek to determine what he wants to achieve. His identification of an aim will take into account many factors including the objectives and capabilities of the belligerents as well as a realistic appraisal of what is feasible. In practice the initial aim may be no more than to get competing factions to meet; it may well be refined as the meeting progresses. Specific preparations will include researching the background and history of the issue to be discussed, taking into account all previous relevant reports. The negotiator or mediator should conduct a survey of those arguments that the belligerent parties may wish to deploy. Options, limitations, minimum requirements and areas of common interest and possible compromise should be identified. If negotiating, the Wider Peacekeeper should be clear on those points he must win or protect and those that may be used as bargaining chips. He should also make a thorough study of the participants who will attend the meeting including their cultural origin, personality, authority, influence, habits and attitudes. If hosting the meeting, specific arrangements should take account of the following:

    a. *Location*. The site of the negotiations or mediation should be secure and neutral.

b. *Administration.* Administrative organization should include such things as arrival and departure arrangements, and the provision of parking, communications, meals and refreshments. Vehicles of the Wider Peacekeeping force may often be the only means of transporting delegates to and from meetings. This transport requirement may demand considerable time and effort. The meeting itself will require an agenda, a seating plan and note-takers, perhaps supplemented with interpreters and other specialist advisers on such subjects as weapons, unexploded ordnance, economics, culture and religion. Meetings may continue for considerable periods of time and commanders should expect to have to feed all those who attend. Administrative details are important and may make a considerable difference to the attitudes of the participants.

c. *Attendance.* Attendance should be at an appropriate and equal rank level. Great offence may be caused if senior representatives from one faction are required to meet with junior representatives from another. To avoid unmanageable numbers attending, the size of each party should be specified and checked. What weapons can and cannot be brought into the meeting should also be announced in advance. Rules for bodyguards must be established and Wider Peacekeeping commanders should bring their own bodyguards with them. Protocol must be paid particular attention.

10. **Conduct.** In the case of mediation, parties to the conflict will confer with the go-between in separate locations. Negotiations, on the other hand, will be held openly in one location with all the participants present. Although it may be extremely difficult, the first item on the agenda should be for the participants to agree the purpose of the meeting. If hosting the occasion, the Wider Peacekeeper should remember to offer the customary salutations and exchange of courtesies and to ensure that all parties are identified and have been introduced to each other. Refreshments should normally be proffered or received. Some introductory small talk is useful and polite on such occasions to make everybody feel at ease and assess the mood. The following principles should guide negotiation itself:

a. *Preserve Options.* The opposing sides should be encouraged to give their views first. This will enable the negotiator to re-assess the viability of his own position. If possible, he should avoid taking an immediate stand and he should be wary of making promises or admissions unless the situation absolutely calls for it.

b. *Restraint and Control.* Belligerent parties are often likely to prove deliberately inflexible. They may distort information shamelessly and introduce red-herrings to distract attention from areas that might embarrass them. Nonetheless, visible frustration, impatience or anger at such antics may undermine the negotiator's position. Cheap 'point-scoring' (even if valid) may achieve short-term gain by embarrassing or discrediting another party. In the longer term, however, such gain will invariably be paid for many times over in terms of forfeited goodwill. Loss of face is likely to increase the belligerence of faction leaders. Simple face-saving measures by the controlling authority will probably act in the longer term interests of all parties. Whenever possible, therefore, respect should be shown for the negotiating positions of other parties. Speakers should not normally be interrupted. Incorrect information should be corrected, if necessary with appropriate evidence. Facts should take preference over opinions.

    c.   *Argument*. If necessary, the negotiator should remind participants of previous agreements, arrangements, accepted practices and their own pronouncements. However, this should be done tactfully and with scrupulous accuracy. It may be appropriate to remind participants that they cannot change the past but, if they wish, they have the power to change the future.

    d.   *Compromise*. Partial agreement or areas of consensus should be carefully explored for compromise solutions. Related common interests may offer answers to seemingly intractable differences.

    e.   *Closing Summary*. Negotiation and mediation should be finalized with a summary of what has been resolved. This summary must be agreed by all participants and, if possible, written down and signed by the principals. A time and place for further negotiation should also be agreed.

11.   **Follow-up**. Effective follow-up is every bit as important as successful negotiation. Without a follow-up, achievements by negotiation or mediation will be meaningless. The outcome of the negotiations or mediation must be promulgated to all interested parties. Background files should be updated with all pertinent information, including personality profiles of the participants. Agreements must be monitored, implemented or supervised as soon as possible. The immediate period following a negotiated agreement is likely to prove the most critical. To preserve the credibility of the negotiating process, what has been agreed must happen and any breach of agreement should be marked at the very least by immediate protests.

12.   **Individual Qualities**. The individual qualities and personality of the negotiator or mediator play a most important rôle. If negotiating, beyond the immediate interests of the issue under discussion he must remain scrupulously impartial. If mediating, the trust he requires of each party to the conflict demands that he demonstrate absolute impartiality and discretion at all times. He should continually take care to avoid giving away information or confidences about third parties which may be of value to their opponents. He must be firm, fair and friendly - with a mastery of detail, tact, patience, a sense of proportion, resourcefulness and objectivity. On matters of principle he must be insistent without being belligerent. He should never lie or adopt an arrogant or patronizing manner. He should maintain the highest level of dress and deportment at all times.

13.   **Languages**. A correct mix and distribution of language skills will be a fundamental element of planning for negotiations. Commanders should be practised in the art of using an interpreter.

14. **Summary**. Negotiation and mediation are critical techniques in Wider Peacekeeping operations. Their aim is conciliation. All opportunities for negotiation or mediation should be explored and fully exploited to encourage belligerents to arrive at mutually agreed solutions to their problems. The importance of negotiation and mediation skills should be emphasized by commanders at all levels and the skills should be practised to the full.

LIAISON

15. **Introduction**. Conflict thrives on rumour, uncertainty and prejudice. The timely passage of accurate information based on a trusting relationship is a key method of combating uncertainty and promoting stability in a conflict region. Liaison is therefore a vital tool of a Wider Peacekeeping force and key to the successful execution of operations. Failure to liaise risks misunderstanding, friction, opposition and escalation of the conflict.

16. **Purpose**. The purpose of liaison is to ensure the timely passage of information, to notify intentions, lodge protests, coordinate activity, manage crises and settle disputes. A liaison system is therefore required to link the Wider Peacekeeping force, the communities, the civil authority (if it exists) and the parties to the conflict. It should be established at every possible level including formation, unit, sub-unit and sometimes below that. The specialist skills and background experience of liaison officers should, if possible, match those of the organization with which they are to liaise. The most effective form of liaison is that of an individual who is permanently detached from his parent organization to the group or faction with which the organization is liaising. Alternative methods of liaison include patrols, regular or occasional meetings and visits.

17. **Requirements**. The liaison individual or team will require robust, reliable communications with an alternative back-up system. In situations of particular tenseness, consideration should be given to creating 'hot lines' linking force command posts with that of opposing factions in order to facilitate the handling of crises. Liaison must be founded on friendly, working relationships. Team members should familiarize themselves with the names and responsibilities of the leaders they deal with. They should also assess attitudes and attempt to predict and anticipate the direction that events may take. Everything should be done to foster an atmosphere of trust. Daily meetings should be arranged (if necessary 'off the record') to develop relationships and keep open channels of communication.

18. **A Priority**. Opportunities for liaison should be explored and exploited by commanders as a priority at every level. It will normally be necessary for commanders to augment their establishments with additional officers, warrant officers and senior NCOs for liaison purposes. If liaison is interrupted for any reason, commanders should seek to re-establish it at the earliest opportunity.

CIVIL AFFAIRS

19. **Limitations of Force**. As Chapter Two has discussed, without a reasonable level of local support, Wider Peacekeeping operations are likely to prove largely fruitless in the long term. Unless the general backing of the local populace can be gained, the security of Wider Peacekeeping personnel and non-governmental organizations, as well as the safety of their bases and movement, is likely to be jeopardized. In such circumstances a recourse to the use of force is made more likely. But, the use of force is most unlikely to persuade uncooperative elements of a population to submit enduringly to the conditions of a peace agreement. In a Wider Peacekeeping environment, coercion is thus a limited and short-term means of engendering cooperation. Firepower is consequently not normally an effective tool for resolving conflicts - indeed, in the long term, violent coercion is likely to foster resentment, hostility and, ultimately, armed opposition.

20. **A Longer-Term Approach**. By contrast, winning the hearts and minds of the local population by a sustained civil affairs programme can transform the security environment and permit the safe accomplishment of a wide range of tasks inherent to Wider Peacekeeping operations. Civil affairs campaigns thus establish the basis for a longer-term, more integrated process which relies less on the explicit use of force and more on fostering local support for the Wider Peacekeeping objectives. The accomplishment of a popular civil affairs campaign may therefore prove a critical element of success.

21. **Civil Affairs Projects**. Civil affairs projects may embrace a wide range of activities within local communities including medical and veterinary care, the provision and distribution of water, waste disposal, electrical power, the removal of unexploded ordnance, the restoration of public services and the construction and development of schools and civil aid centres. Such projects will invariably entail the commitment of specialist resources including engineers, medical, veterinary, military police and special forces elements and are likely to require extensive logistic support. In undertaking projects, the advice of government, non-governmental organizations and relief agencies should be sought and programmes should be coordinated locally. However, civil affairs projects will lose their effectiveness if conducted in isolation. Priorities should therefore be coordinated at formation level and integrated into the theatre-wide plan. All elements of the Wider Peacekeeping force should be seen to be supporting such programmes in a coherent and consistent way. Commanders should allocate generous resources to civil affairs projects. The "hearts and minds" return will amply justify such investment. The prevailing attitudes of the local population towards the Wider Peacekeeping force is a matter of considerable importance and commanders should anticipate and exploit civil affairs opportunities to the full.

PUBLIC INFORMATION

22. **Significance**. Wider Peacekeeping operations, particularly at the outset, are likely to attract intense public scrutiny via the international media. Their reports, influencing as they do widespread psychological perceptions, will have a signifi-

cant impact on the direction and course of operations. Media reports may restrict or promote a force's freedom of action. A timely introduction of press reporters to the scene of a crisis may serve to restrict belligerents' actions and forestall atrocity. If managed effectively, media attention can enhance a contingent's overall prospects of success by making appropriate messages widely known. An informed and educated public is more likely to respond maturely to major crises within a Wider Peacekeeping operation. Any void in information is likely to be filled with the propaganda of opposing factions, fuelled by media speculation. An effective public information service is therefore an essential element of Wider Peacekeeping operations. Public information demands the personal attention of the commander and should be treated as integral to the operation. The public information organization should be integrated into the mainstream command, control and reporting systems of the Wider Peacekeeping force.

23. **Principles**. The community information principles described above apply to public information. The following are additional principles that should govern public information support:

   a. *Accreditation*. Media representatives should normally be accredited in order to gain eligibility for public information support. The accreditation should require them to abide by a clear set of basic ground rules that protect the operational security of the Wider Peacekeeping force. If the rules are violated, consideration should be given to excluding offenders from access to further public information services.

   b. *Openness*. Open and independent reporting should be the norm. In most situations, unrestricted access should be allowed to accredited media. Warnings of dangers specific to certain areas should be given but should not preclude media access. Threats to personal security are an occupational hazard of media representatives. They are ultimately responsible for the consequences of the risks they take.

   c. *Quality of Service*. Public information support should be prompt, accurate, balanced and consistent

   d. *Liaison*. Public information liaison upwards and downwards within the Wider Peacekeeping force is essential at all times. Given the potential for political repercussions, higher authority should be kept informed of all significant developments in media reporting. Several public information staff should be available at unit level for detachment to incidents at short notice.

COMMUNITY INFORMATION

24. **Terminology**. The psychological dimension of Wider Peacekeeping operations is a prominent and critical element of campaign activity that deserves the closest attention. It is minds that have to be changed. Any means of influencing perceptions, particularly those of the parties to the conflict, will be of crucial importance. Community information therefore plays a vital rôle in Wider Peace-

keeping. There is a clear distinction between community information and public information. The latter builds attitudes in a world-wide context and is governed by the agenda of the media. Community information targets selected audiences and is a direct tool of the commander. It is, in effect, psychological operations under a gentler and more acceptable name.

25. **Aim.** Community information aims to influence the emotions, perceptions, motives, objective reasoning and ultimately the behaviour of target audiences. It represents for the commander a non-lethal means of engendering compliance and cooperation within his area of operations. Specifically, community information seeks to promote popular support and discourage armed opposition. It attempts to portray an honest representation of the competence, credibility, resolve, achievements and human face of the Wider Peacekeeping force whilst also emphasizing the responsibility of local nationals to resolve their own differences. It seeks to educate and enlighten. Community information may additionally undertake a coordinating function including the broadcast of warnings, future intentions of the controlling authorities and details of agreements reached between opposing factions. In all, community information has the potential to make significant contributions to the overall conflict resolution process. Its planning should start early and form part of the commander's overall plan.

26. **Principles.** The following general principles should govern the application of a community information campaign:

    a.   *Impartiality.* The neutrality of the Wider Peacekeeping force must be repeatedly stressed. Nothing should be communicated that might prejudice the force's perceived impartiality. The 'enemy' is anarchy, atrocity and starvation.

    b.   *Cultural Knowledge.* A thorough understanding of local culture, including dialects, is vital. Active effort must be made to gain this understanding. Socio-cultural studies and opinion surveys should be conducted to identify prevailing attitudes and expose misconceptions and misunderstandings that can then be addressed through the community information campaign.

    c.   *Coordination and Integration.* As a psychological activity, community information projects must be coordinated and integrated with other activities that seek to determine and influence perceptions. These will include military information, civil affairs projects and public information. Other operational elements that might be required to support community information activities will include aviation and electronic warfare assets.

    d.   *Truth.* Unless the information promulgated is believed, community information will serve no purpose. Demonstrable truth must therefore be the stock-in-trade of community information material. Exposed lies or evident propaganda will impose profound damage to the long term credibility and viability of any community information programme.

e.	*Style*. Community information material should be presented as public service announcements and must avoid appearing patronizing, arrogant or blatantly manipulative.

27.	**Targets and Means**. Targets for community information activities are likely to include elements of the Wider Peacekeeping force itself, all sections of the populace, parties to the conflict, local civilian and military authorities, non governmental organizations, media, relief agencies, and private voluntary organizations. All potential means of undertaking community information activity should be carefully assessed. There may well be extensive local resources such as radio stations that could be used. Such resources should be preserved and not destroyed. As well as radio and television broadcasts, community information material may be disseminated by loudspeaker broadcasts, leaflet drops, information sheets and newspapers. The most effective means of all, however, may prove to be community relations open days (see below) and regular face-to-face information briefings with local leaders.

28.	**Resources Required**. Effective community information will require sizeable resources including media, technical, linguistic, cultural and regional specialists. Such personnel will normally be grouped into production teams (to cover research and the production of radio, video and printing materials), dissemination teams (with mobile audio-visual and loudspeaker resources) and liaison teams to coordinate and link supporting agencies.

COMMUNITY RELATIONS

29.	**Nature and Purpose**. Community relations, as an element of both the public information and community information programmes, refers to the deliberate fostering of social contact with the indigenous population. The purpose of community relations is to create favourable perceptions locally and encourage cooperative responses to the Wider Peacekeeping force's activities. Community relations, by its actions, seeks to convey implicitly simple but positive messages such as: "Trust us", "We are here to help you" and "Peace is the only way ahead".

30.	**Conduct**. Community relations may be developed through formal occasions such as sports days, musical concerts, displays, recreational outings, and tea parties. Such occasions may be large or small. Community relations activities may also be conducted at a low level on a daily basis by small and specialized teams which are able to provide local interest and entertainment in various ways. Community relations occasions should avoid being blatantly manipulative - relaxed informality should normally set the tone. Nevertheless, such occasions should be carefully planned and executed, and undue security risks must be avoided. Community relations programmes should not be conducted in a way that might prejudice the Wider Peacekeeping force's perceived impartiality. All elements of the local population should be included.

SECTION THREE - MANAGEMENT TECHNIQUES

MILITARY INFORMATION

31. *Terminology*. The parties to a conflict in a Wider Peacekeeping environment will be suspicious of all intelligence-related activities. They are likely to regard the gathering of intelligence itself as a hostile act. The standard function of intelligence in Wider Peacekeeping is therefore termed 'military information'. This terminology seeks to accommodate local sensitivities as well as those that may exist within a multinational Wider Peacekeeping force itself.

32. *The Information Process*. Although the impartial context of Wider Peacekeeping is different from that of conventional military operations, the principles which guide military information techniques are similar to those that govern the operational intelligence function. The significance of military information in Wider Peacekeeping operations is no less than that of intelligence in conventional operations. Military information will drive the conduct of Wider Peacekeeping operations and is the direct responsibility of the commander. As an operational function, military information will represent a prime influence in directing and synchronizing operations themselves. Military information works through the continuous cyclical process of direction, collection, interpretation, evaluation, collation and dissemination. The information organization must be flexible and task organized and will probably require considerable augmentation to include specialists in a wide variety of fields.

33. *Information Requirements*. The information requirements of the commander in Wider Peacekeeping are likely to be broader and more complex than those of normal combat operations. There will be no "enemy" - only conflicting factions. As well as requiring detailed assessments of the geopolitical situation including historical and cultural influences, the commander will also require continuously updated assessments of the attitudes and capabilities of all local forces, ethnic groupings and interested parties to the conflict - particularly those that are potentially hostile. This will include detailed profiles of leading personalities in their areas of responsibility. In addition, the information organization should monitor all events and aspects of the general security environment that are volatile and have the potential to escalate violence at short notice.

34. *Sources*. Much of the data required will be available from open source material including libraries, the media, multinational business corporations and commercial satellite services. Other sources of information will include assessments from higher formation as well as those from national and regional authorities. At the tactical level, a primary source of military information will be reports and routine debriefings of those elements of the force that are deployed as well as local nationals and NGOs. NGOs are particularly useful sources of information.

35. *Summary*. A well-developed information system is vital to the effectiveness of Wider Peacekeeping operations. Military information must be directed by the commander to meet clearly defined requirements to satisfy operational needs. In

addition, the military information organization will meet a vital early warning requirement in monitoring and reporting those aspects that may destabilize or escalate the overall security situation. The rôle of military information in planning Wider Peacekeeping operations is covered in more detail in Chapter Six.

OBSERVATION AND MONITORING

36. Observation is a fundamental element of Wider Peacekeeping operations. Its purpose is to gather information, and monitor, verify and report adherence to agreements of any kind, thus deterring and providing evidence of breaches. Examples of observation tasks include the following:

    a. Observing Buffer Zones and Ceasefire Lines.

    b. Confirming the withdrawal of forces.

    c. Monitoring conditions in a potential conflict area for signs of war preparation or increased tension.

    d. Monitoring and reporting human rights abuses.

    e. Inspecting industrial facilities to verify compliance with UN Security Council Resolutions.

    At levels of reduced tension, observation may be carried out by unarmed personnel in small multinational teams, often including civilian representatives. At higher levels of tension, observers may be lightly armed and grouped in single-nationality military teams. Methods used by observers might include the manning of static observation posts and checkpoints as well as foot and vehicle patrols. Effective liaison with all parties involved is a critical element of most of these methods. The success of observation activities depends largely on accurate, timely reporting using reliable communications. By their nature, observation and monitoring teams are normally limited in the scope of reactive action they can take themselves.

INTERPOSITION

37. *Introduction.* As during the Cold War, the interposition of forces between opposing factions remains one of the basic military tasks in peacekeeping operations and applies particularly to the establishing and maintenance of ceasefires within the context of demobilization operations. In these circumstances it is usually pre-planned with the consent of belligerent parties and normally follows (but could precede) the withdrawal and assembly of opposing factions from a ceasefire line. The interposition might be phased with advance groups deployed to provide a screen between withdrawing factions. Such groups might take the form of standing patrols or armoured vehicles. Interposition in this situation should be accomplished as quickly as possible to forestall clashes which might lead to a breakdown of the ceasefire arrangements. Interpositioned forces may be required to protect the parties to a conflict from outside interference and attack, as well as taking action against the violators of ceasefires.

38. ***Emergency Response***. Interposition may also be used as a short-term emergency response to forestall or manage a local crisis. As with a pre-planned interposition, speed is a crucial factor in defusing such a situation. If the early stages of a crisis appear manageable, commanders should promptly attempt to insert leading elements of an interpositional force between the parties concerned, whilst concurrently conducting immediate negotiations with the antagonists at the point of physical confrontation. While negotiations continue to reduce tension and the danger of violence, the interpositional group should be reinforced until the latter is sufficiently strong to regain control of the situation. Care should be taken not to escalate crises by such action.

39. ***Demobilization Operations***. An interpositional force in demobilization operations will normally need to be similar in composition to that required for a preventive deployment including armoured protection and possibly indirect fire assets. As in preventive deployment, an interpositional force will require the availability of reinforcements to bolster its credibility and provide support in emergencies. Opposing factions may attempt to attack or pass through interpositioned forces. The principles governing the use of force in self-defence therefore apply directly to an interpositioned group and must be fully understood and applied as necessary.

40. ***Credibility***. Interposition may prove a hazardous operation but its capacity to separate antagonists makes it a valuable and rewarding operational technique. Interposition should only be used, however, when the force concerned is operationally credible. The interpositional force will serve little purpose if its size is such that it can be easily pushed aside or neutralized by opposing factions.

SUPERVISION

41. In Wider Peacekeeping operations supervision is an activity that would normally occur within the framework of interposition. Supervision assignments will cover all stages of demobilization operations including the withdrawal, disarming, relocation, disassembly and rehabilitation of military or paramilitary parties to a conflict. Supervisory tasks will include negotiating and planning, the process of withdrawal and disarmament, and promulgating the essential information in time to allow the parties to respond. Supervision also includes the investigation of complaints and alleged breaches of agreement. Whenever possible, supervisory tasks should be conducted by local civil authorities rather than Wider Peacekeeping forces. It may also be possible to delegate certain supervised tasks jointly to the parties to a conflict. If linked to appropriate rewards and penalties, such action would encourage their joint cooperation. Delegating supervisory tasks in this way is risky and would require tight control. However, if feasible, it could contribute significantly towards the conciliation of the parties concerned.

CONTROL MEASURES

42. ***Sectors***. The best means of exerting control in Wider Peacekeeping operations is the allocation to commanders of responsibility for geographical areas of operation. Accordingly, the operational area should be broken down into sectors

allocated and sub-allocated to formations, units and sub-units. If possible sector boundaries should take account of political and civil authority borders, the location of ethnic groups and parties to the conflict, and significant geographical features.

43. ***Guards and Checkpoints***. Within the framework of sectors, military operations will usually require control to be established either to monitor, limit or deny access to many areas including:

Key terrain (such as Ceasefire Lines, Buffer Zones and Control Zones)
Installations
Centres of population
Stocks of war supplies.

This may be achieved by the use of guards (for the custody and accounting of war supplies, for example) and checkpoints. Checkpoint requirements and the procedures and tactics they employ will depend on the provisions and authority of the mandate, the Status of Forces Agreement and the Wider Peacekeeping force Standing Operational Procedures. Guards and checkpoints may constitute a major interface between the peacekeeping contingent and local populace. It is therefore key that soldiers carrying out such duties should be scrupulous in their observation of good manners and local custom, particularly in dealing with women. Patience and courtesy must be applied to safeguard the sense of personal esteem and collective honour which dominates individual and group behaviour in many foreign communities.

44. ***Powers of Search and Arrest***. The powers of the Wider Peacekeeping military force to search and arrest civilians will depend on the mandate and Status of Forces Agreement. In a Wider Peacekeeping situation, such powers are likely to be a necessary adjunct to controlling actions taken by the force. Control will need to be exerted over the passage of war supplies. Preventative action may also be needed to combat the smuggling of contraband items such as drugs. In the early stages of a demobilization operation, UN troops may be empowered to confiscate items and arrest offenders. In a military assistance phase, civilians or faction members suspected of illegal activity will usually be handed over to the civil authorities. Checks on the personnel and vehicles of the Wider Peacekeeping force may also be appropriate to demonstrate that the force itself is observing the law and to deter or detect any criminal activity among its own members.

45. ***Crowd Control***. In a military assistance situation, a Wider Peacekeeping force may be committed to supporting the civil authority in controlling a public assembly. The armament, number of troops deployed and scale of reserves will depend on the situation. Reconnaissance, deployment of reserves, liaison with the civil authority and minimum force will be critical factors guiding the execution of such a control measure.

PATROLLING

46. ***Introduction and Application.*** Patrolling is likely to prove a key activity in Wider Peacekeeping operations. If well-planned, vigorous and intelligent in execution, patrolling can contribute much to the tactical initiative sought by commanders. Patrolling has many applications:

    a. *Information gathering.* Patrols may be organized to confirm or supplement information provided by static observation posts or other means. Reconnaissance of inaccessible or dangerous areas may be carried out at long range by specialist troops in armoured vehicles.

    b. *Security.* Patrols can provide additional security when complementing guards or checkpoints. They may also be used as escorts to representatives of the Wider Peacekeeping force, relief agencies or aid convoys as well as the civil authority or threatened elements of the local populace.

    c. *Other Tasks.* Patrolling can also be used to carry out aspects of most Wider Peacekeeping operational tasks including mobile checkpoints, investigation, interposition, supervision, liaison, negotiation and 'flying the flag' to reassure and calm troubled areas, deter law-breakers and promote the credibility and prestige of the Wider Peacekeeping force.

47. ***Means.*** Patrols may be conducted by day or night in all conditions of climate and terrain. They may be carried out on foot or by any alternative means that might be available including soft-skinned and armoured vehicles, fixed or rotary wing aircraft and sea vessels. The protection of the patrol in the prevailing situation will be a key factor in determining the means to be used.

CHAPTER SIX

PLANNING FOR OPERATIONS

"The end crowns all,
And that old common arbitrator, Time,
Will one day end it."

William Shakespeare

SECTION ONE - INTRODUCTION

1. ***Context***. In defining success in Wider Peace-keeping operations, Section Nine of Chapter One emphasised that military action could not be viewed as an end in itself, but would rather complement diplomatic, economic and humanitarian endeavours which together would pursue political objectives. The Wider Peacekeeper, therefore, does not plan for victory. Such a concept would be inappropriate and, in predicating itself on an unrealisable goal, would flaw the planning process. Planning Wider Peacekeeping operations must therefore recognise and take into account the subordination of operations to diplomatic and humanitarian activity - and the likely effect of such subordination on military objectives. Achieving the strategic end-state will be the principal criterion of plans. Details of the decision-making and planning process are in ADP "Command".

> **CONTENTS**
>
> INTRODUCTION
>
> PLANNING PROCESS
>
> MISSION ANALYSIS
>
> FACTORS
>
> TASKS AND PRINCIPLES
>
> TECHNIQUES
>
> CONCEPT OF OPERATIONS
>
> DIRECTIVES AND ORDERS

2. ***Purpose***. The purpose of this chapter is to review planning methods for Wider Peacekeeping operations, including the estimate process, and identify the principal concerns that need to be addressed.

SECTION TWO - PLANNING PROCESS

3. ***Introduction***.

   a. *Operational Context*. At the commencement of operational level planning the Head of Mission (HoM), normally the Special Representative of the Secretary General (SRSG), should aim to translate the Security Council mandate into a 'campaign' plan with an unambiguous concept of operations and a clearly defined end-state. The HoM should produce the 'campaign' plan jointly with the Force Commander and the senior representatives of the lead UN civil agency and of an 'umbrella' agency representing the NGOs. The 'campaign' plan should allocate resources, specify military, diplomatic and humanitarian missions and establish their linkage and coordination. Coordination mechanisms will need to reflect that coordination of NGOs can only be by consent and not by direction. Campaign planning for UN operations, as far as possible, should cater for possible subsequent changes to the operational mandate.

b. *Planning Process.* Military operations at the tactical level should be planned within the overall context of the HoM's 'campaign' plan and in the knowledge that at all levels operations will need to be coordinated with other involved agencies. Planning for Wider Peacekeeping operations at the tactical level will normally involve the following:

Preliminary assessment
Reconnaissance
Liaison
Estimate

The planning stages described above are neither consecutive nor separate. Some of them are likely to take place concurrently and the overall process may repeat itself cyclically and in varying orders.

4. **Preliminary Assessment.** Nearly all planning activities will be preceded by a period of preliminary assessment which may, in the early stages, represent little more than contingency planning. The preliminary assessment is likely to take many different forms and will include all types of research drawing on the widest source of materials. At this stage the commander should identify his information requirements and establish the structures necessary for collection, processing and dissemination. See also paragraphs 25-28.

5. **Reconnaissance.** Reconnaissance has no substitute and will always pay. The direct observation of conditions on the ground combined with face-to-face liaison with other agencies is critical to effective planning. Reconnaissance should therefore be undertaken as soon as possible and involve the maximum number of the commander's key personnel in order that their own areas of interest might be effectively covered.

6. **Liaison.** The broad nature of Wider Peacekeeping operations means that the planning of military and civil activities must be conducted in concert from the beginning. Military planners should therefore liaise at the earliest possible opportunity with all related military contingents, civil agencies and NGOs in order to ensure that their planned intentions are synchronised and in harmony with the wider aspects of operational activity. Such liaison should be a continuous process.

7. **Estimate.** The commander's estimate (or appreciation) represents the most important planning element. It is, in effect, the commander's overall assessment of his own sphere of responsibility - an assessment that will determine the nature and conduct of his operational activities and direct their execution. Because Wider Peacekeeping will be politically dynamic the commander must remain alert to the

affects of all changes of mandate, however minor, continually reviewing and revising his estimate and all that devolves from it. The estimate is a cyclical process involving the stages depicted in the following diagram:

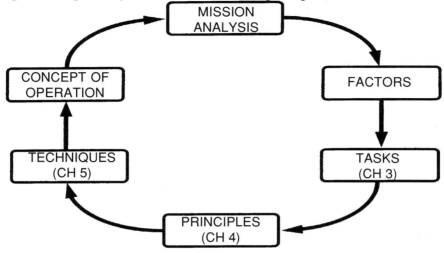

The remainder of this chapter will cover each of the estimate's steps shown in the diagram.

SECTION THREE - MISSION ANALYSIS

8. ***Mission***. Starting with an appropriate and clearly defined mission is key to the estimate process. Commanders should check carefully that their mission is adequately defined and resourced. Ideally, the mission given to the commander should cover what to achieve, where, when and why - but not how.

9. ***Analysis***. The commander must then analyse the mission given him in the light of his commander's concept of operations. This analysis should therefore ensure that all plans are consistent in the immediate and long term with the commander's future intentions and the overall strategic requirements. Such a plan should avoid encouraging any actions that are inconsistent with those requirements or that may foreclose longer term plans.

SECTION FOUR - FACTORS

10. ***Introduction***. This Section will not review all factors that need to be taken into account when planning. Factors such as time and space are self-evident in their application and need no further explanation. What follows, therefore, is not an exhaustive checklist, but rather a review of those factors especially relevant to Wider Peacekeeping operations and which merit special consideration.

11. ***Parties to the Conflict***. Commanders must make an accurate and thorough assessment of the parties to the conflict within their operational areas. This assessment will probably need to embrace a wide range of military, paramilitary and civilian groups and will require careful analysis of their political and military

aspirations, motives, organisations, strength, weapons, equipment, doctrine, leadership, training, discipline and general attitudes and stability. Such analysis should lead to an overall view of the parties' strengths, weaknesses and likely intentions and activities. Their past record of honouring agreements and cease-fires will be a critical element of this assessment.

12. *Operational Environment*. The operational environment of Wider Peacekeeping will include tangible and intangible aspects. The former will encompass topography, including lines of communication, climate, the general living conditions, ethnic distribution, languages, religion and customs of the populace. The national infrastructure of the area and the potential influence of neighbouring regions should also be taken into account. Intangible elements of the operational environment will include the indigenous population's culture, psyche and attitude as well as public perceptions of the conflict, both locally and world-wide. The potential for sudden and unexpected escalations in violence and the level of conflict would also come into this category. The intangible elements are likely to exert a key influence on the Wider Peacekeeping force's activity and general deportment. An effective assessment of the operational environment will demand a close study of the general history of the region as well as the origins and nature of the conflict.

13. *Allocation of Resources*. The allocation of manpower, equipment and the level of sustainability will have significant bearing on the character of the campaign to be conducted. The availability of reserves and reinforcements to commanders will also be important factors in planning. Planners should take account of the availability of local resources and host nation support and make full use of these where it would not deprive the local population of essential supplies.

14. *Restrictions and Obligations*. The mandate, Rules of Engagement, Status of Forces Agreement, as well as national and international laws, conventions and agreements will probably severely restrict the conduct of operations. These factors must be very carefully assessed and it is likely that commanders will require clarification from their higher authority on many of the aspects concerned.

15. *Multiplicity of Participation*. The commander should make a careful assessment of other agencies operating within his area of responsibility. As well as joint and multinational elements, other agencies might include governmental and non governmental organisations and private voluntary organisations. Planning should take full account of the identity, rôle, interests, intentions and methods of these agencies and the need for the Wider Peacekeeping force to harmonise activities as much as possible.

SECTION FIVE - TASKS AND PRINCIPLES

16. *Assessment of Tasks*. Having analysed his mission and taken full account of relevant factors, the commander's next step will be to identify and assess the tasks that have to be carried out to achieve his mission. These tasks may be both specified and implied. The commander must abandon all preconceptions in this process and seek to adopt fresh perspectives on the requirements as they appear.

It may be that tasks which might be taken for granted prove on reflection to be unnecessary, whilst tasks that appear at first sight to be of fringe benefit actually turn out to be essential. Included in the commander's assessment of tasks will be that of providing a contingency reserve to cope with unexpected developments including sudden escalations in violence. If appropriate, such a force should be of multinational composition in order to demonstrate the international resolve of the Wider Peacekeeping force. Having identified the necessary tasks, the commander should then prioritise them in terms of importance. He should also identify those tasks that may be carried out concurrently, and those that may only occur sequentially. In the case of the latter, he should determine the order in which the tasks need to be carried out. They are discussed at length in Chapter Three.

17. **Principles.** Before deciding which techniques to employ in undertaking the identified tasks, the commander should carefully review the principles, specific to his situation, that should guide his choice of techniques. Again, preconceptions must be resisted and radical reflection may produce fresh and unusual perspectives which could lead planning down avenues that might not normally be explored. Principles are an essential link between tasks and techniques in Wider Peacekeeping. They are discussed at length in Chapter Four.

SECTION SIX - TECHNIQUES

18. **Introduction.** Having reached this stage, the commander is now ready to consider, choose and prioritise the techniques that the Wider Peacekeeping force will employ in carrying out the necessary tasks. Operational techniques have already been covered in Chapter Five. This Section therefore highlights some of the planning considerations related to a number of the key techniques.

19. **Command.** The complexity and sensitivity of Wider Peacekeeping create unique problems for command. Exacerbated by media presence, the atmosphere of a Wider Peacekeeping operation is likely to be highly charged politically and strategic and operational level considerations will tend to bear down to the lowest level. There will therefore be a tendency for the operational and tactical levels of command to overlap as individual incidents assume a high profile in political terms via the news media. The tactical commander will suffer additional limitations if operating in a multinational and multiagency environment. Each national contingent is likely to have separate national command arrangements which will affect many aspects of operations - particularly if sudden and unexpected escalations of violence occur.

20. **Liaison.** Chapter Five has emphasised the critical importance of effective liaison to co-ordinate the divergent activities of the many parties and agencies likely to be involved in Wider Peacekeeping operations. Liaison requirements and arrangements must be assessed and planned at the very earliest opportunity. The establishment of a comprehensive liaison network will require the presence of capable liaison personnel at a wide range of locations, including the local offices of the pertinent civil agencies, as well as the headquarters of the parties to the conflict. Plans should take into account the need for liaison teams to be

independent logistically, particularly with regard to transport and communications. Arrangements may also have to include the provision of interpreters who will require careful selection, briefing and training.

21. **Coordination**. Planning should consider all means available to coordinate effectively operational activities within a Wider Peacekeeping force. These means will include Standing Operational Procedures which commanders will receive from their superior authority and which will require interpretation for use at lower levels. They will also serve to assist the commander in ensuring correctness and commonalty in approach to such matters as Rules of Engagement, public information and general conduct. Coordination between civil and military agencies may be managed by regular meetings at all appropriate levels, as well as normal liaison arrangements.

22. **Communications**. When developing communications plans, the use of civil means of communications, if reliable, should be considered. However, sole reliance and dependency on host nation systems must be avoided. Mobility and reliability will be key characteristics of the communications required by many elements of the Wider Peacekeeping force, particularly observation and liaison teams. The size and terrain of the operational area may itself pose communications problems.

CONSENT TECHNIQUES

23. **Emphasis**. Wider Peacekeeping is concerned with conflict resolution, not termination, and the consent techniques that address the mind and perceptions of the public are therefore likely in the long term to contribute more directly to success than most of the management techniques. Planning should therefore take account of this and, within the establishment of a reasonable security framework, lend emphasis to consent operational techniques. Such psychological methods have the additional benefit of being non-lethal - again an aspect more consistent with the overall ethos of Wider Peacekeeping. The planning and execution of consent techniques should therefore be given command emphasis from the very beginning.

24. **Conduct**. Consent techniques will tend to overlap in their effects on public perceptions and will therefore require continual and careful co-ordination to ensure that a coherent and consistent message is being produced. Commanders should plan to take a direct and close interest in this and ensure that the necessary liaison both within and between the appropriate agencies is being carried out. The style in which consent techniques are employed will be all-important and their planning and execution should therefore reflect the principles described in Chapter Four.

MILITARY INFORMATION

25. **Introduction**. Military information must always form the foundation of the commander's decisions. The planning, design and operation of military information systems, as Chapter Five has already emphasised, should therefore be

command-driven. Operational techniques will support military information systems in creating a widespread interface between members of the Wider Peacekeeping force and the local population. Whilst outside of military control NGOs may also prove useful sources of information.

26. **Information Requirements**. In planning his Wider Peacekeeping military information system, the commander must identify his information requirements and the task organisation needed to satisfy such requirements. In addition to general data concerning the operational environment (including terrain and weather), the tactical commander's information requirements for Wider Peacekeeping operations are likely to seek answers to the following questions:

   a. *Conflict* - What are the root causes of the conflict at the local level and how might they be alleviated?

   b. *Belligerent Parties* - What are the belligerent parties' capabilities, future intentions, morale and discipline? What are the profiles of their leading personalities? What external influences bear on their actions?

   c. *Volatility* - What is the potential for escalation in violence? Why, when and where is such escalation likely to occur?

   d. *Demography* - What is the ethnic distribution and attitude of the local population? What part will they play in future operations and how might they best contribute to the conflict resolution process?

27. **Information Resources**. Having identified his information requirements, the commander will then be able to plan his collection, processing and dissemination activities. This procedure will enable him to estimate the appropriate military information assets he will need, including augmentation requirements. Depending on the level of command, a wide range of information specialists are likely to be needed, including area experts, linguists, analysts, interrogators and security personnel. This should be planned well in advance of deployment, and the personnel involved should be assembled together and practised beforehand.

28. **Multinational Environment**. In a multinational environment information may need to be shared with other nations. Appropriate security caveats and dissemination criteria should therefore be agreed beforehand with the commander's superior authority. Liaison and exchange appointments within a multinational force will be important to encourage a commonalty of approach to military information and a sharing of the product.

SECTION SEVEN - CONCEPT OF OPERATIONS

29. **Introduction**. The final stage of the planning process is the production of a concept of operations. In effect, this is the commander's plan which organises and co-ordinates the application of those operational techniques that have been identified in the previous stage. The concept of operations represents the logical

culmination of the previous stages - the analysis of the mission followed by a detailed consideration of all factors, tasks, principles and techniques. As the fruit of the planning process, the concept of operations will reflect the balance and priorities of the commander's estimate. It will identify where the main effort of operations should lie. The concept of operations will determine the missions and co-ordinating instructions that the commander will give to his subordinates, and the task organisation and service support he will allocate to enable his subordinates to execute those missions.

30. **Phases**. The concept of operations should cover the phases listed below. Allowances must be made within each phase for changes in the nature of operational environment and activity.

    a.   *Preparation*. The preparation phase covers all activities prior to departure, including warning, reconnaissance, planning, liaison, assembly, administration and training. Training for Wider Peacekeeping is covered in Chapter Seven.

    b.   *Deployment*. The deployment phase starts with the departure of the Wider Peacekeeping force from its home base and ends with its arrival in the theatre of operations.

    c.   *Operations*. The operational phase begins with the arrival of the force in theatre and covers their reception, their move to base camp, preparatory measures, the force's tactical deployment forward into the operational area of responsibility and the conduct of operations. Establishing the force's security and self-sufficiency will be prime planning considerations in the early stages. Preparation will include briefings, reconnaissance, liaison visits, training, and administration. If taking over from other troops, the force's tactical deployment forward may be conducted as a relief in place operation. Once the supporting operational infrastructure is established and working, Wider Peacekeeping operations will begin

    d.   *Redeployment*. The redeployment phase starts with the cessation or handing over of operational tasks. The nature of redeployment may vary from emergency extraction to planned withdrawal or routine roulement. Redeployment will cover the transfer of all operational and administrative activities to relieving troops, international relief agencies or national authorities. All aspects of such transfer must be anticipated, fully co-ordinated before redeployment begins, and executed in a speedy and efficient manner. Time for redeployment may be limited and plans for this stage of operations must be flexible and capable of adaptation to different situations at short notice. Post operational activities will embrace all after-action activity, including post operational reports, the submission of lessons learned data and administration.

31. **Resources**. In considering the employment of his various resources, the commander's concept of operations should take into account the following particular special to arm capabilities:

a.   *Infantry*. Infantry will normally represent the most significant component of the Wider Peacekeeping force. Infantry are suited to hold positions, provide presence and observation, man checkpoints and conduct patrols. Armoured personnel vehicles will enhance their protection and employability for such tasks as interposition.

b.   *Armour*. Tanks may not be appropriate or practical in most Wider Peacekeeping operations. However, armoured reconnaissance units are particularly useful, especially when a unit's geographical area of responsibility is large. The firepower, mobility, protection and communications of armoured reconnaissance vehicles suits them for such tasks as liaison, control points, convoy security, quick reaction and proving routes.

c.   *Aviation*. Helicopter aviation units may perform a range of essential functions in Wider Peacekeeping including reconnaissance, surveillance, liaison, transport and medical evacuation.

d.   *Special Forces*. The characteristics of special forces have many pertinent applications to Wider Peacekeeping scenarios. Their ability to be deployed discreetly at long range with secure communications renders special forces capable of short notice liaison, reconnaissance and assessment tasks. Special forces are also suited to civil affairs, community relations and community information activities as well as the raising, training and reform of indigenous irregular armed groups and host nation security forces.

e.   *Engineers*. A principal engineer mission is likely to be the support of civil affairs programmes. This might include the supply or maintenance of civil infrastructure facilities such as the provision of shelters, waste disposal facilities and electrical power, and the procurement, storage and distribution of water. Engineers will also be able to supervise the location, removal and disposal of mines and other unexploded ordnance. Mobility is another important task for engineer resources, especially in such operations as the protection of the delivery of humanitarian relief supplies. Engineer representatives should be included in reconnaissance parties.

f.   *Artillery*. In a preventive deployment, artillery may fill a deterrent role as well as providing a contingency capability in responding to unexpected and uncontrolled escalations of violence. In the guarantee and denial of movement (probably coordinated at the operational level of command) artillery - particularly air defence may be used to enforce a no-fly zone. However, the deployment and use of fire support assets may prove inappropriately provocative in most of the conflict resolution activities of Wider Peacekeeping operations. That said, there may still be uses in Wider Peacekeeping for mortar and artillery illumination, as well as locating radars - the latter for documenting and apportioning blame for violation of ceasefire agreements.

g.   *Military Police*. In Wider Peacekeeping military police detachments are able to perform security tasks, control measures, and to undertake general police duties. In the sensitive environment of military assistance tasks, military police can work in close cooperation with host nation civil police and assist in the maintenance of law and order. They may also be used to detect and curtail possible illegal activities (such as black marketeering) by any members of the Wider Peacekeeping force.

32.   **Troops to Task**. Having assessed the required tasks and the preferred techniques to accomplish them, the commander's next logical step will be to allocate his available resources to those tasks. This calculation should be done for each phase of the operation and will determine which activities may be done concurrently and which (owing to the requirement to concentrate resources) will need to be undertaken sequentially. This process will provide a general overview of what is operationally feasible and set prudent limits on the commander's aspirations. The commander's troops to task calculation will thus determine the overall shape of his concept of operations.

33.   **Grouping and Missions**. The Wider Peacekeeping commander will then group his resources and allocate missions to each grouping. This action is the culmination of the operational planning process. It should reflect the emphasis and priorities of the deductions derived from all preceding stages of the commander's estimate. In articulating missions for their own subordinates groupings, commanders should take full account of the widest ramifications of the mission given them - which in Wider Peacekeeping will embrace diverse diplomatic, economic and social factors. The principle of coherence described in Chapter Four should be applied and the missions devised should be such that survive short term developments and maximise the scope for exploiting the conditions of the mandate. Groupings must be task organised and tailored to the allocated missions. The characteristics of each grouping, including structure, equipment and training standards must be appropriate to the tasks it will undertake and should also allow for contingencies. If possible, groups should be flexible, self-contained and able to meet their own security requirements. Groupings should specify and authorise augmentation requirements including that of liaison personnel and interpreters.

34.   **Reserves**. The volatility of most Wider Peacekeeping environments demands that special attention be given to the creation of reserves at each level of command. As well as demonstrating resolve, possible reserve tasks include preventive deployment, reinforcement, and the protected extraction of other elements of the force. Reserve forces should be uncommitted, mobile, at an appropriate readiness state, and of sufficient strength to represent a credible reaction force.

COMBAT SERVICE SUPPORT (CSS)

35.   **Introduction**. Wider Peacekeeping will pose unique and significant challenges to the CSS function. The operational environment may be characterised by long distances, difficult terrain, a hostile climate, and a dearth of basic facilities and host

nation support. Meeting CSS demands will therefore be a complex and demanding process, requiring careful planning. Indeed, CSS considerations are likely to dictate major aspects of the Wider Peacekeeping force's modus operandi. CSS advisers must be involved at the start of the planning process and be included in reconnaissance. The early deployment of CSS assets is desirable whenever possible. Typically, Wider Peacekeeping units may be expected to deploy with personal weapons and ammunition, organic transport, communications, equipment support and medical assets, and sufficient stocks of all basic supplies to last at least 30-90 days.

36. **CSS Directive**. As in his troops to task process, the commander must balance and match his CSS requirements against his resources. Having done so, he will formulate his CSS directive, clearly stipulating his logistic priorities, both in terms of which types of support are the most critical and which customers have the highest priority. He must also take full and careful account of any CSS limitations which may impinge upon his future intentions and contingency plans. Invariably, CSS demands will constrain the scope of operations and may sometimes require the commander's overall planning process to be repeated and revised.

37. **CSS Functions**. CSS functions include supply, repair, equipment support, medical, provost and welfare services. The CSS organisation will need the capacity to adapt and adjust its efforts, and the merits of centralising or decentralising sustainment must be assessed according to the situation. If deployed over long distances, it may be appropriate for sub units to have their own supporting CSS detachments. CSS operations that support other military forces or cross multinational boundaries will require extensive liaison. Wider Peacekeeping operations may demand the commitment of CSS resources to support civil affairs programmes for the benefit of the indigenous population. Such commitments might include medical support, health care, veterinary assistance and extensive construction projects. If engaged in the latter, engineers are likely to require frequent and large supplies of construction materials. Careful coordination between engineer and supply or contract units will be essential. Given the likely need to exploit local resources, the operation of contracting agencies will be of particular significance to CSS activity.

SECTION EIGHT - DIRECTIVES AND ORDERS

38. The end result of the planning cycle is direction which leads to execution. Directives and orders provide the principal means by which the intentions of the commander are conveyed to his subordinates. Details on the production and dissemination of directives and orders can be found in ADP "Command".

CHAPTER SEVEN

TRAINING

"Custom call me to 't:
What custom wills, in all things should we do't...."
William Shakespeare

SECTION ONE - INTRODUCTION

1. ***Reference Material***. This Chapter will not furnish a comprehensive and detailed checklist of points to be covered in training for Wider Peacekeeping. For such guidance commanders are referred to Army Training Directives which set out training standards required in conventional military skills. These skills are foundational to the successful execution of Wider Peacekeeping tasks. In addition, detailed guidance for Wider Peacekeeping training may be gainedfrom AFM Vol V Part 1 'Peacekeeping Operations' and the UN Department of Peacekeeping Operations publication 'Peace-Keeping Training - Training Guidelines and Exercises' issued through the chain of command. Commanders should carefully review these references in preparing for Wider Peacekeeping missions.

> ### CONTENTS
>
> INTRODUCTION
>
> TRAINING PLAN
>
> INDIVIDUAL TRAINING
>
> > Conceptual Approach
> > Orientation
> > Special Skills
>
> COLLECTIVE TRAINING

2. ***Importance of Training***. The Wider Peacekeeping environment is likely to be complex, dangerous and stressful, placing heavy demands on all individuals participating in field operations. The point of contact between the belligerent parties and the Wider Peacekeeping force will frequently be the young soldier or NCO. It is often at this level that crisis situations may be held in check and resolved. Alternatively, it is at this level that crises can escalate and get out of control, thus threatening to destabilize the immediate environment - an effect that may easily spread to other areas. It is therefore of critical importance that each member of a Wider Peacekeeping force is both psychologically prepared and militarily trained for his tasks and the environment in which they will be carried out. Training for such operations must be realistic and progressive and take full account of their special nature. Training is the direct responsibility of the commander.

3. ***A Continuous Process***. Training is not confined to preparing troops before deployment. It is a continuous ongoing process which constantly seeks to refresh and hone skills. Wider Peacekeeping tasks may often prove repetitive and tedious, thus eroding readiness and morale. A constructive ongoing cycle of in-theatre training will prevent boredom, raise morale, develop unit cohesion and maintain operational effectiveness. Training in theatre may also serve to maintain visibility and demonstrate resolve without being unnecessarily provocative.

4. ***Education as a Foundation***. Training derives from doctrine. Doctrine therefore provides the intellectual underpinning which imparts meaning to actions. Effective training thus requires a clear explanation of theory to precede the practice of its application. Education is therefore a critical element of training and theoretical classroom study will precede the practice of most Wider Peacekeeping skills. Soldiers who understand the long-term purpose of their activities are likely to perform their duties more effectively than those who do not. Understanding allows individuals at the most junior level to exercise initiative and flexibility to the full in order to exploit opportunities. In complex and volatile environments, the understanding and attitude of each Wider Peacekeeper will therefore be critical to the effective performance of his duties. A comprehensive educative process is thus the most important element of training and foundational to preparing for Wider Peacekeeping tasks.

5. ***Peacekeeping Ethos***. Rather than terminating conflict by force, the Wider Peacekeeper's task is to resolve conflict in the rôle of an impartial third party supervisor. This calls, above all, for an adjustment of the soldier's attitude and approach which will differ markedly from the approach he would normally adopt in carrying out conventional operations. The Wider Peacekeeper will normally be a guest of the host nation, a representative of the UN and a goodwill ambassador of his own nation. The demands of preserving a consensual framework for operations will require him to respect local culture, customs and behaviour. The principles of impartiality, minimum force, legitimacy, credibility, mutual respect and transparency - the peacekeeping 'ethos' - will govern his actions. The need for such an approach must be carefully explained and fully understood by all contingent members.

6. ***Relevance of Basic Military Skills***. Notwithstanding their special nature, Wider Peacekeeping operations will require many of the qualities and training required for conventional operations. Professional competence, discipline, morale, leadership, initiative, flexibility and alertness will remain crucial elements of a contingent's operational effectiveness. Training for Wider Peacekeeping therefore requires a thorough grounding in basic military skills including such things as command, control and communications, navigation, weapon handling, tactical skills, physical training and administration.

SECTION TWO - THE TRAINING PLAN

7. ***Identifying the Requirement***. Every Wider Peacekeeping situation will be unique. It is the commander's responsibility to identify the specific training requirement of his own operational task. This will derive from his preliminary assessment, reconnaissance, liaison and estimate - the operational planning process described in Chapter Six. Standing Operational Procedures of the superior formation and post operation tour reports of other units will assist the commander in identifying the training requirement. Reasonable scope should be allowed for the expected operational task to develop and change. When complete, the training requirement should specify what subjects need to be understood and practised by whom and in what order of priority. Training requirements and

standards will influence the commander's operational planning throughout the contingent's tour of duty.

8.   **Factors**. Several factors will influence the development of the training requirement and its translation into a training plan. At this stage commanders should take careful account of the existing training standards of all individuals who will come under their command on deployment. They should also consider the resources that will be available for training, particularly time and facilities (including instructors and training aids) and existing courses. Innovative consideration should be given to such things as preparatory reconnaissance, liaison, attachments and detachments, exchanges, the formulation of training teams and other means of expanding and developing training resources.

9.   **Training Plan**. The commander's training plan will specify how the training requirement will be met. It must be flexible and take all pertinent factors into account. The training plan should specify the general allocation of available time and cover in-theatre activities as well as pre-deployment preparation.

SECTION THREE - INDIVIDUAL TRAINING

10.   **Introduction**. Individual training is the basis of a contingent's collective effectiveness. Its foundation is the education that will impart an overall perspective and understanding of the Wider Peacekeeping task and that will precede any practical application of operational techniques. This Section will describe in outline those subjects which should be considered for inclusion in an individual training programme. The individual training requirement is classified under three categories:

Conceptual Approach
Orientation
Special Skills

CONCEPTUAL APPROACH

11.   **The UN**. Essential background to any Wider Peacekeeping training is a general understanding of the material covered in Chapters 1 - 4 of this manual. All members of a contingent should be aware of the UN's rôle, general organization, operation and Charter. In addition, individuals should have explained to them, illustrated with appropriate case studies, the pragmatic development of peacekeeping and the fundamental principles which guide its conduct. Relevant aspects of national and international law should also be covered, as well as appropriate provisions of the Geneva Convention.

12.   **Philosophy, Principles and Techniques**. Fundamental to an intelligent appreciation and application of operational techniques is an understanding of the Wider Peacekeeping philosophy described in Chapter 2. This should emphasize the prime significance and nature of consent - and its doctrinal interpretation in terms of impartiality and minimum necessary force. The remaining principles and operational techniques described in Chapters 3 and 4 should also be the subject of classroom instruction.

13. ***Qualities Required.*** The general effect of background training should be to highlight the qualities required of members of a Wider Peacekeeping contingent. In the field of operations the activities of each individual should be characterized by professional, disciplined conduct seasoned with practical commonsense, a flexible outlook, patience, restraint, tact, a good sense of humour, vigilance and an objective approach. The aggressive pursuit of "victory" and disparaging public comments about the belligerent parties or the contingents of other nations must be understood as entirely inappropriate.

ORIENTATION

14. ***Geopolitical and Cultural Background.*** In addition to grasping the necessary conceptual approach, the Wider Peacekeeper will require comprehensive briefing relating to the particular operation he will undertake. Such orientation should include the geography and climate of the region, its economic and military situation in outline and the political background, origins and course of the dispute in question. Each soldier needs to be made aware of the political motivations, government structure, history, religion, customs, ethnic lifestyles and social structures of the indigenous population and the different factions in the dispute to which he will be a third party. Only when he has understood the causes of the dispute and the perspectives of those involved in it can he adjust his attitude and approach to the requirements of the situation and to the rôle that he will perform. Cultural factors may determine tiny but important details of the Wider Peacekeeper's conduct including expression, voice tone, touch and distance when dealing with the parties to the conflict and members of the local population. Prior to deployment, consideration should be given to procuring FCO or diplomatic representatives to brief on the progress of recent UN resolutions, what politicians are trying to achieve in theatre, the national line being taken, and on the reception of any recent peace initiatives.

15. ***Hazards, Recognition and Languages.*** Orientation briefings should also cover local security, health and hygiene hazards and recognition of the uniforms, rank insignia, equipment, weapons, vehicles and aircraft of the belligerent parties and indigenous security forces. All ranks should also be taught useful phrases of the local languages such as greetings, thanks, and sentry challenging procedures, including the word to halt. Ideally, all contingent members should be provided with a phrase book containing key words or phrases in the native languages of the area of operations.

16. ***Mandate and Protocols.*** The Wider Peacekeeping mandate, Status of Forces Agreement and other relevant protocols must be carefully reviewed and interpreted to explain how they affect the rights, privileges, duties and methods of operation of the contingent. Commanders and staff officers will require to study these documents closely. All members of the Wider Peacekeeping force should have clearly explained to them the scope afforded and limits placed on their actions by the mandate, Status of Forces Agreement, protocols and laws under which they operate. This area of orientation will inevitably be complex and require frequent refresher training and practised application using hypothetical scenarios. This training will continue in theatre after deployment.

17. **Non-Governmental Organizations**. The general nature, rôle, organization and modus operandi of non-governmental and private voluntary organizations operating in the contingent's area should also be described in briefings. Individuals should be made aware of the relationship and status that members of such organizations have with regard to the Wider Peacekeeping force. If possible, relevant agencies should be asked to visit and brief units before those units deploy.

18. **Administration**. Whilst operational training will of course take precedence, administrative education and awareness is important to the effectiveness of a Wider Peacekeeping contingent. Administrative briefings should therefore be included within training packages. Subjects covered should include pay, allowances, conditions of service, inoculations, leave, rest and recreation, domestic arrangements for families, post, canteen and currency.

SPECIAL SKILLS

19. Special training will be required to supplement conventional military skills with those particular Wider Peacekeeping skills identified in the commander's training plan. Training should therefore include coverage of the following special skills:

   a. *Law of Armed Conflict*. All members of the contingent must be made aware of the rules they must observe to comply with The Law of Armed Conflict. Army Training Directive Number 2 details the necessary reference material and minimum training requirements for soldiers, NCOs and officers. This training should be supplemented by briefings on any Arms Control agreements or negotiations relevant to the theatre concerned. Officers should familiarize themselves with the appropriate elements of the Geneva Conventions, including such things as the status of refugees and displaced persons.

   b. *Use of Force*. The principle of minimum force is covered in Chapter 3. It must be clearly and completely understood by all peacekeepers. The entire contingent should be thoroughly familiar with alternatives to the use of force and the principles that should govern its employment. They should understand the scope and limits imposed by Rules of Engagement and what action has to be taken after force has been used. This aspect of special training should be practised as frequently as possible, both formally and informally, using such methods as discussion of varying hypothetical scenarios, as well as general question and answer sessions.

   c. *Negotiation, Mediation and Liaison*. All members of a Wider Peacekeeping force may find themselves in an emergency situation which will require them to negotiate, mediate or liaise with members of the belligerent factions or local population. This subject should therefore be covered by all ranks although those specifically selected to fulfil such rôles as liaison officers will require considerable extra training. The use of interpreters should be practised

   d. *Community and Public Information*. Whilst community and public information activities are likely to be the province of specialists, all members of the contingent have a part to play in giving correct and appropriate impressions to the media and local community and should be briefed accordingly.

e. *Military Information.* All ranks will contribute to the collection of military information and should be taught and practise what to look out for and how to report it

f. *Civil Affairs.* Civil affairs programmes will normally be the province of specialist personnel such as engineers and assault pioneers who may require extensive training in minefield clearance, EOD, building construction and the installation of services such as water, power and sanitation. All contingent members should be briefed as to the importance of civil affairs programmes and their contribution to developing relationships with the community and resolving conflicts

g. *Mine Awareness.* Wider Peacekeepers will normally be deployed to the vicinity of former battlefields. They may, therefore, be exposed to old minefields and other types of dangerous battlefield debris. In addition, new mines may be laid by the belligerent parties. An assessment of the mine risk must therefore be made and training may have to be conducted emphasizing detection, recognition and reporting. Instructors may have to be trained to conduct minefield awareness training for local civilians

h. *Observation and Monitoring.* Observation and monitoring will be a primary task for many members of the Wider Peacekeeping contingent. The training syllabus should include the siting, defence and construction of observation posts, daily routine, the maintenance of logs and use of standardized reporting formats, observation techniques for searching ground by day and night, and the operation of surveillance equipment

i. *Interposition and Control Measures.* The tactics, requirements and procedures for interposition and control measures will depend on the provisions and authority of the mandate, Status of Forces Agreement and Force Standing Operational Procedures. Training should cover subjects like the siting and layout of checkpoints as well as detailed procedures to respond to such things as the discovery of contraband, refusal to produce identification or submit to searching, the brandishing of firearms and crashing through of barriers. Crowd control techniques may also be appropriate subjects for training

j. *Supervision.* Training for supervisory actions should be conducted in the context of demobilization operations and include such things as the investigation of complaints, the procedures for which will be laid down in Force Standing Operational Procedures

k. *Patrolling.* Training for patrol duties (including escorts) should cover all types of patrol, their purpose and conduct

l.   *NBC*. NBC may well be a feature of the Wider Peacekeeping environment - either through industrial accidents or sabotage, or the use by belligerents of NBC weapons. NBC training is likely therefore to constitute an important element of preparatory training

m.   *Standing Operational Procedures*. All individuals should have a working knowledge of Force, contingent and unit Standing Operational Procedures. If available in time, they may be used to direct many aspects of pre-deployment training. Ideally each soldier should have a personal aide-memoire which will contain the pertinent information required to perform his duty

n.   *Health*. Wider Peacekeeping operations will often be conducted in areas and climates where diseases are prevalent due to primitive sanitary conditions, lack of medical facilities, or the effects of the conflict. Individuals should be trained to maintain their health and to take preventive action in basic health care, hygiene and sanitation. If the climate of the operational theatre differs significantly from that of the home base, acclimatization will be an important element of preparation following deployment

o.   *Medical Training*. A sizeable proportion of unit personnel (perhaps one crew member per vehicle) should be trained to well above the basic requirements of Army Training Directive Number 5. Practical aspects of that training should approach Regimental Medical Assistant 3 standard. Numerous battle handling exercises should be used to validate theoretical medical training.

p.   *Recognition Training*. The recognition of appropriate fixed wing aircraft, helicopters and ground vehicles should be practised. Basic recognition training should include repeated 'crack and thump' demonstrations to develop and practise the ability to identify a broad variety of types and calibre of weapons

q.   *High Frequency (HF) Communications*. HF communications may often prove of critical importance to Wider Peacekeeping. Consideration should therefore be given to training appropriate numbers (again, perhaps one member of each vehicle crew) in the proficient use of HF

r.   *Safety*. The safety of troops should be of continuous concern to commanders. Training in safety precautions should cover the following areas:

   (1)   *Construction of Shelters*. Each position should include a shelter to accommodate personnel in that area, including extra space for visitors

   (2)   *Movement Security*. Contingent members may be at special risk when travelling. Training should therefore cover such things as vehicle security measures, avoidance of routine, route selection, defensive driving, counter hijack drills and anti-ambush drills

(3) *Road Safety.* Traffic accidents are one of the largest causes of death on peacekeeping operations. Training should therefore emphasize safety on the road and cover host nation traffic regulations. All drivers should be competent in driving across country and on sheet ice. Negotiating narrow tracks, roads and bridges should be practised. Drivers of armoured fighting vehicles must be confident of their ability to drive closed down for long periods and manoeuvre in confined spaces

(4) *Weapon Handling.* Soldiers will probably handle their personal weapons and live ammunition more often than in normal peacetime activities. Over-familiarity and fatigue may cause needless accidents and training must continually emphasize safe weapon handling drills. Basic training should also be conducted in the use of former Warsaw Pact small arms, particularly unloading and making safe

s. *Helicopter Drills.* If helicopters are to be used in theatre, pre-deployment training should include safety briefings and the practice of all drills, including emplaning, deplaning, crash and casualty evacuation.

SECTION FOUR - COLLECTIVE TRAINING

20. **Introduction.** The purpose of collective training is to validate individual training standards and practise the corporate performance of what has been learnt. Collective training affords broad scope for exploring issues, widening individuals' perspectives, increasing understanding and developing practical skills. It will also develop team cohesiveness and promote morale.

21. **Methods.** The number of ways in which collective training may be conducted is limited only by the commander's imagination. It may be conducted at any level and with any grouping of individuals. Collective training methods will include the following:

a. *Discussion Groups.* Directed discussions of topics can range from formal seminars to informal question-and-answer sessions. The composition of groups may also range from gatherings of commanders or particular specialists to formed groupings of any variety. Visitors with particular experience or knowledge may be included.

b. *Command Post Exercises.* Command post exercises may be used to test and practise command, control and communications at all levels, addressing every phase of likely operations, including logistics and UN staff procedures.

c. *Gaming and Simulation.* At its most sophisticated, gaming and simulation may be carried out using computer-based operational analysis. At more basic levels, useful training experience may be gained from playlets and rôle-playing exercises which seek to enact particular scenarios which require to be resolved.

d.   *Field Training Exercises.* Field training exercises may be carried out at any level. They will particularly suit the exercise of skills required by large-scale activities such as preventive deployment and demobilization operations.

22.   **Conduct**. Soldiers will become discouraged if unfamiliar skills are exercised on a scale and intensity beyond their abilities. Although realism is desirable, collective training should be conducted in a progressive fashion that takes proper account of existing training standards. When conducting pre-deployment training, commanders should seek to have the administrative support for that training delegated to other units in order that their own troops may gain the maximum benefit.

CHARTER OF THE UNITED NATIONS

INTRODUCTORY NOTE

1. The Charter of the United Nations was signed on 26 June 1945, in San Francisco, at the conclusion of the United Nations Conference on International Organization, and came into force on 24 October 1945. The Statute of the International Court of Justice is an integral part of the Charter.

2. Amendments to Articles 23, 27 and 61 of the Charter were adopted by the General Assembly on 17 December 1963 and came into force on 31 August 1965. A further amendment to Article 61 was adopted by the General Assembly on 20 December 1971, and came into force on 24 September 1973. An amendment to Article 109, adopted by the General Assembly on 20 December 1965 came into force on 12 June 1968.

3. The amendment to Article 23 enlarges the membership of the Security Council from eleven to fifteen. The amended Article 27 provides that decisions of the Security Council on procedural matters shall be made by an affirmative vote of nine members (formerly seven) and on all other matters by an affirmative vote of nine members (formerly seven), including the concurring votes of the five permanent members of the Security Council.

4. The amendment to Article 61, which entered into force on 31 August 1965, enlarged the membership of the Economic and Social Council from eighteen to twenty-seven. The subsequent amendment to that Article, which entered into force on 24 September 1973, further increased the membership of the Council from twenty-seven to fiftyfour.

5. The amendment to Article 109, which relates to the first paragraph of that Article, provides that a General Conference of Member States for the purpose of reviewing the Charter may be held at a date and place to be fixed by a two-thirds vote of the members of the General Assembly and by a vote of any nine members (formerly seven) of the Security Council. Paragraph 3 of Article 109, which deals with the consideration of a possible review conference during the tenth regular session of the General Assembly, has been retained in its original form in its reference to a "vote, of any seven members of the Security Council", the paragraph having been acted upon in 1955 by the General Assembly, at its tenth regular session, and by the Security Council.

CHARTER OF THE UNITED NATIONS

WE THE PEOPLES OF THE UNITED NATIONS DETERMINED

to save succeeding generations from the scourge of war, which twice in our lifetime has brought untold sorrow to mankind, and

to reaffirm faith in fundamental human rights, in the dignity and worth of the human person, in the equal rights of men and women and of nations large and small, and

to establish conditions under which justice and respect for the obligations arising from treaties and other sources of international law can be maintained, and

to promote social progress and better standards of life in larger freedom,

AND FOR THESE ENDS

to practice tolerance and live together in peace with one another as good neighbours, and

to unite our strength to maintain international peace and security, and to ensure, by the acceptance of principles and the institution of methods, that armed force shall not be used, save in the common interest, and

to employ international machinery for the promotion of the economic and social advancement of all peoples,

HAVE RESOLVED TO COMBINE OUR EFFORTS TO ACCOMPLISH THESE AIMS

Accordingly, our respective Governments, through representatives assembled in the city of San Francisco, who have exhibited their full powers found to be in good and due form, have agreed to the present Charter of the United Nations and do hereby establish an international organization to be known as the United Nations.

CHAPTER I

PURPOSES AND PRINCIPLES

Article 1

The Purposes of the United Nations are:

1.   To maintain international peace and security, and to that end: to take effective collective measures for the prevention and removal of threats to the peace, and for the suppression of acts of aggression or other breaches of the peace, and to bring about by peaceful means, and in conformity with the principles of justice and international law, adjustment or settlement of international disputes or situations which might lead to a breach of the peace;

2.   To develop friendly relations among nations based on respect for the principle of equal rights and self-determination of peoples, and to take other appropriate measures to strengthen universal peace;

3.   To achieve international co-operation in solving international problems of an economic, social, cultural, or humanitarian character, and in promoting and encouraging respect for human rights and for fundamental freedoms for all without distinction as to race, sex, language, or religion; and

4.   To be a centre for harmonizing the actions of nations in the attainment of these common ends.

Article 2

The Organization and its Members, in pursuit of the Purposes stated in Article 1, shall act in accordance with the following Principles.

1.   The Organization is based on the principle of the sovereign equality of all its Members.

2.   All Members, in order to ensure to all of them the rights and benefits resulting from membership, shall fulfil in good faith the obligations assumed by them in accordance with the present Charter.

3.   All Members shall settle their international disputes by peaceful means in such a manner that international peace and security, and justice, are not endangered.

4.   All Members shall refrain in their international relations from the threat or use of force against the territorial integrity or political independence of any state, or in any other manner inconsistent with the Purposes of the United Nations.

5.   All Members shall give the United Nations every assistance in any action it takes in accordance with the present Charter, and shall refrain from giving assistance to any state against which the United Nations is taking preventive or enforcement action.

6.   The Organization shall ensure that states which are not Members of the United Nations act in accordance with these Principles so far as may be necessary for the maintenance of international peace and security.

7.   Nothing contained in the present Charter shall authorize the United Nations to intervene in matters which are essentially within the domestic jurisdiction of any state or shall require the Members to submit such matters to settlement under the present Charter; but this principle shall not prejudice the application of enforcement measures under Chapter VII.

CHAPTER II

MEMBERSHIP

Article 3

The original Members of the United Nations shall be the states which, having participated in the United Nations Conference on International Organization at San Francisco, or having previously signed the Declaration by United Nations of 1 January 1942, sign the present Charter and ratify it in accordance with Article 110.

Article 4

1.   Membership in the United Nations is open to all other peace-loving states which accept the obligations contained in the present Charter and, in the judgment of the Organization, are able and willing to carry out these obligations.

2.   The admission of any such state to membership in the United Nations will be effected by a decision of the General Assembly upon the recommendation of the Security Council.

Article 5

A Member of the United Nations against which preventive or enforcement action has been taken by the Security Council may be suspended from the exercise of the rights and privileges of membership by the General Assembly upon the recommendation of the Security Council. The exercise of these rights and privileges may be restored by the Security Council.

Article 6

A Member of the United Nations which has persistently violated the Principles contained in the present Charter may be expelled from the Organization by the General Assembly upon the recommendation of the Security Council.

CHAPTER III

ORGANS

Article 7

1.   There are established as the principal organs of the United Nations: a General Assembly, a Security Council, an Economic and Social Council, a Trusteeship Council, an International Court of Justice, and Secretariat.

2.   Each subsidiary organs as may be found necessary may be established in accordance with the present Charter.

Article 8

The United Nations shall place no restrictions on the eligibility of men and women to participate in any capacity and under conditions of equality in its principal and subsidiary organs.

CHAPTER IV

THE GENERAL ASSEMBLY

Composition

Article 9

1.   The General Assembly shall Consist of all the Members of the United Nations.

2.   Each Member shall have not more than five representatives in the General Assembly.

Functions and Powers

Article 10

The General Assembly may discuss any

questions or any matters within the scope of the present Charter or relating to the powers and functions of any organs provided for in the present Charter, and, except as provided in Article 12, may make recommendations to the Members of the United Nations or to the Security Council or to both on any such questions or matters.

Article 11

1.   The General Assembly may consider the general principles of co-operation in the maintenance of international peace and security, including the principles governing disarmament and the regulation of armaments, and may make recommendations with regard to such principles to the Members or to the Security Council or to both.

2.   The General Assembly may discuss any questions relating to the maintenance of international peace and security brought before it by any Member of the United Nations, or by the Security Council, or by a state which is not a Member of the United Nations in accordance with Article 35, paragraph 2, and except as provided in Article 12, may make recommendations with regard to any such questions to the state or states concerned or to the Security Council or to both. Any such question on which action is necessary shall be referred to the Security Council by the General Assembly either before or after discussion.

3.   The General Assembly may call the attention of the Security Council to situations which are likely to endanger international peace and security.

4.   The powers of the General Assembly set forth in this Article shall not limit the general scope of Article 10.

Article 12

1.   While the Security Council is exercising in respect of any dispute or situation the functions assigned to it in the present Charter the General Assembly shall not make any recommendation with regard to that dispute or situation unless the Security Council so requests.

2.   The Secretary-General, with the consent of the Security Council, shall notify the General Assembly at each session of any matters relative to the maintenance of international peace and security which are being dealt with by the Security Council and shall similarly notify the General Assembly, or the Members of the United Nations if the General Assembly is not in session, immediately the Security Council ceases to deal with such matters.

Article 13

1.   The General Assembly shall initiate studies and make recommendations for the purpose of:

a.   promoting international co-operation in the political field and encouraging the progressive development of international law and its codification;

b.   promoting international co-operation in the economic, social, cultural, educational, and health fields, and assisting in the realization of human rights and fundamental freedoms for all without distinction as to race, sex, language, or religion.

2.   The further responsibilities, functions and powers of the General Assembly with respect to matters mentioned in paragraph 1(b) above are set forth in Chapters IX and X.

Article 14

Subject to the provisions of Article 12, the General Assembly may recommend measures for the peaceful adjustment of any situation, regardless of origin, which it deems likely to impair the general welfare or friendly relations among nations, including situations resulting from a violation of the provisions of the present Charter setting forth the Purposes and Principles of the United Nations.

Article 15

1.   The General Assembly shall receive and consider annual and special reports from the Security Council; these reports shall include an account of the measures that the Security Council has decided upon or taken to maintain international peace and security.

2.   The General Assembly shall receive and consider reports from the other organs of the United Nations.

Article 16

The General Assembly shall perform such functions with respect to the international trusteeship system as are assigned to it under Chapters XII and XIII, including the approval of the trusteeship agreements for areas not designated as strategic.

Article 17

1.   The General Assembly shall consider and approve the budget of the Organization.

2.   The expenses of the Organization shall be borne by the Members as apportioned by the General Assembly.

3.   The General Assembly shall consider and approve any financial and budget-ary arrangements with specialized agencies referred to in Article 57 and shall examine the administrative budgets of such specialized agencies with a view to making recommendations to the agencies concerned.

Voting

Article 18

1.   Each member of the General Assembly shall have one vote.

2.   Decisions of the General Assembly on important questions shall be made by a two-thirds majority of the members present and voting. These questions shall include: recommendations with respect to the maintenance of international peace and security, the election of the non-permanent members of the Security Council, the election of the members of the Economic and Social Council the election of members of the Trusteeship Council in accordance with paragraph 1(c) of Article 86, the admission of new Members to the United Nations, the suspension of the rights and privileges of membership, the expulsion of Members, questions relating to the operation of the trusteeship system, and budgetary questions.

3.   Decisions on other questions, including the determination of additional categories of questions to be decided by a two-thirds majority, shall be made by a majority of the members present and voting.

Article 19

A Member of the United Nations which is in arrears in the payment of its financial contributions to the Organization shall have no vote in the General Assembly if the amount of its arrears equals or exceeds the amount of the contributions due from it for the preceding two full years. The General Assembly may, nevertheless, permit such a Member to vote if it is satisfied that the failure to pay is due to conditions beyond the control of the Member.

Procedure

Article 20

The General Assembly shall meet in regular annual sessions and in such special sessions as occasion may require. Special sessions shall be convolved by the Secretary-General at the request of the Security Council or of a majority of the Members of the United Nations.

Article 21

The General Assembly shall adopt its own rules of procedure. It shall elect its President for each session.

Article 22

The General Assembly may establish such subsidiary organs as it deems necessary for the performance of its functions.

CHAPTER V

THE SECURITY COUNCIL

Composition

Article 23

1.   The Security Council shall consist of fifteen Members of the United Nations. The Republic of China, France, the Union of Soviet Socialist Republics, the United Kingdom of Great Britain and Northern Ireland, and the United States of America shall be permanent members of the Security Council. The General Assembly shall elect ten other Members of the United Nations to be non-permanent members of the Security Council, due regard being specially paid, in the first instance to the contribution of Members of the United Nations to the maintenance of international peace and security and to the other purposes of the Organization, and also to equitable geographical distribution.

2.   The non-permanent members of the Security Council shall be elected for a term of two years. In the first election of the non-permanent members after the increase of the membership of the Security Council from eleven to fifteen, two of the four additional members shall be chosen for a term of one year. A retiring member shall not be eligible for immediate re-election.

3.   Each member of the Security Council shall have one representative.

Functions and Powers

Article 24

1.   In order to ensure prompt and effective action by the United Nations, its Members confer on the Security Council primary responsibility for the maintenance of international peace and security, and agree that in carrying out its duties under this responsibility the Security Council acts on their behalf.

2.   In discharging these duties the Security Council shall act in accordance with the Purposes and Principles of the United Nations. The specific powers granted to the Security Council for the discharge of these duties are laid down in Chapters VI, VII, VIII, and XII.

3.   The Security Council shall submit annual and, when necessary, special reports to the General Assembly for its consideration.

Article 25

The Members of the United Nations agree to accept and carry out the decisions of the Security Council in accordance with the present Charter.

Article 26

In order to promote the establishment and maintenance of international peace and security with the least diversion for armaments of the world's human and economic resources, the Security Council shall be responsible for formulating, with the assistance of the Military Staff Committee referred to in Article 47, plans to be submitted to the Members of the United-Nations for the establishment of a system for the regulation of armaments.

Voting

Article 27

1.   Each member of the Security Council shall have one vote.

2.   Decisions of the Security Council on procedural matters shall be made by an affirmative vote of nine members.
3. Decisions of the Security Council on all other matters shall be made by an affirmative vote of nine members including the concurring votes of the permanent members, provided that, in decisions under Chapter VI and under paragraph 3 of Article 52, a party to a dispute shall abstain from voting.

Procedure

Article 28

1.   The Security Council shall be so organized as to be able to function continuously. Each member of the Security Council shall for this purpose be represented at all times at the seat of the Organization.

2.   The Security Council shall hold periodic meetings at which each of its members may, if it so desires, be represented by a member of the government or by some other specially designated representative.

3.   The Security Council may hold meetings at such places other than the seat of the Organization as in its judgment will best facilitate its work.

Article 29

The Security Council may establish such subsidiary organs as it deems necessary for the performance of its functions.

Article 30

The Security Council shall adopt its own rules of procedure, including the method of selecting its President.

Article 31

Any Member of the United Nations which is not a member of the Security Council may participate, without vote, in the discussion of any question brought before the Security Council whenever the latter considers that the interests of that Member are specially affected.

Article 32

Any Member of the United Nations which is not a member of the Security Council or any state which is not a Member of the United Nations, if it is a party to a dispute under consideration by the Security Council, shall be invited to participate, without vote, in the discussion relating to the dispute. The Security Council shall lay down such conditions as it deems just for the participation of a state which is not a Member of the United Nations.

CHAPTER VI

PACIFIC SETTLEMENT OF DISPUTES

Article 33

1.   The parties to any dispute, the continuance of which is likely to endanger the maintenance of international peace and security shall, first of all, seek a solution by negotiation, enquiry. mediation, conciliation, arbitration, judicial settlement, resort to regional agencies or arrangements, or other peaceful means of their own choice.

2.   The Security Council shall, when it deems necessary, call upon the parties to settle their dispute by such means.

Article 34

The Security Council may investigate any dispute, or any situation which might lead to international friction or give rise to a dispute, in order to determine whether the continuance of the dispute or situation is likely to endanger the maintenance of international peace and security.

Article 35

1.   Any Member of the United Nations may bridge any dispute, or any situation of the nature referred to in Article 34, to the attention of the Security Council or of the General Assembly.

2.   A state which is not a Member of the United Nations may bring to the attention of the Security Council or of the General Assembly any dispute to which it is a party if it accepts in advance, for the purposes of the dispute, the obligations of pacific settlement provided in the present Charter.

3.   The proceedings of the General Assembly in respect of matters brought to its attention under this Article will be subject to the provisions of Articles 11 and 12.

Article 36

1.   The Security Council may, at any stage of a dispute of the nature referred to in Article 33 or of a situation of like nature, recommend appropriate procedures or methods of adjustment.

2.   The Security Council should take into consideration any procedures for the settlement of the dispute which have already been adopted by the parties.

3.   In making recommendations under this Article the Security Council should also take into consideration that legal disputes should as a general rule be referred by the parties to the International Court of Justice in accordance with the provisions of the Statute of the Court.

Article 37

1.   Should the parties to a dispute of the nature referred to in Article 33 fail to settle it by the means indicated in that Article, they shall refer it to the Security Council.

2.   If the Security Council deems that the continuance of the dispute is in fact likely to endanger the maintenance of international peace and security, it shall decide whether to take action under Article 36 or to recommend such terms of settlement as it may consider appropriate.

Article 38

Without prejudice to the provisions of Articles 33 to 37, the Security Council may, if all the parties to any dispute so request, make recommendations to the parties with a view to a pacific settlement of the dispute.

CHAPTER VII

ACTION WITH RESPECT TO THREATS TO THE PEACE, BREACHES OF THE PEACE, AND ACTS OF AGGRESSION

Article 39

The Security Council shall determine the existence of any threat to the peace, breach of the peace, or act of aggression and shall make recommendations, or decide what measures shall be taken in accordance with Articles 41 and 42, to maintain or restore international peace and security.

Article 40

In order to prevent an aggravation of the situation, the Security Council may, before making the recommendations or deciding upon the measures provided for in Article 39, call upon the parties concerned to comply with such provisional measures as it deems necessary or desirable. Such provisional measures shall be without prejudice to the rights, claims, or position of the parties concerned. The Security Council shall duly take account of failure to comply with such provisional measures.

Article 41

The Security Council may decide what measures not involving the use of armed force are to be employed to give effect to its decisions, and it may call upon the Members of the United Nations to apply such measures. These may include complete or partial interruption of economic relations and of rail, sea, air, postal, telegraphic, radio, and other means of communication, and the severance of diplomatic relations.

Article 42

Should the Security Council consider that measures provided for in Article 41 would be inadequate or have proved to be inadequate, it may take such action by air, sea, or land forces as may be necessary to maintain or restore international peace and security. Such action may include demonstrations, blockade, and other operations by air, sea, or land forces of Members of the United Nations.

Article 43

1.   All Members of the United Nations, in order to contribute to the maintenance of international peace and security, undertake to make available to the Security Council, on its call and in accordance with a special agreement or agreements, armed forces, assistance, and facilities, including rights of passage, necessary for the purpose of maintaining international peace and security.

2.   Such agreement or agreements shall govern the numbers and types of forces, their degree of readiness and general location, and the nature of the facilities and assistance to be provided.

3.   The agreement or agreements shall be negotiated as soon as possible on the initiative of the Security Council. They shall be concluded between the Security Council and Members or between the Security Council and groups of Members and shall be subject to ratification by the signatory states in accordance with their respective constitutional processes.

Article 44

When the Security Council has decided to use force it shall, before calling upon a Member not represented on it to provide armed forces in fulfilment of the obligations assumed under Article 43, invite that Member, if the Member so desires, to participate in the decisions of the Security Council concerning the employment of contingents of that Member's armed forces.

Article 45

In order to enable the United Nations to take urgent military measures, Members shall hold immediately available national air-force contingents for combined international enforcement action. The strength and degree of readiness of these contingents and plans for their combined action shall be determined, within the limits laid down in the special agreement or agreements referred to in Article 43, by the Security Council with the assistance of the Military Staff Committee.

Article 46

Plans for the application of armed force shall be made by the Security Council with the assistance of the Military Staff Committee.

Article 47

1.   There shall be established a Military Staff Committee to advise and assist the Security Council on all questions relating to the Security Council's military requirements for the maintenance of international peace and security, the employment and command of forces placed at its disposal, the regulation of armaments, and possible disarmament.

2.   The Military Staff Committee shall consist of the Chiefs of Staff of the permanent members of the Security Council or their representatives. Any Member of the United Nations not permanently represented on the Committee shall be invited by the Committee to be associated with it when the efficient discharge of the Committee's

responsibilities requires the participation of that Member in its work.

3.   The Military Staff Committee shall be responsible under the Security Council for the strategic direction of any armed forces placed at the disposal of the Security Council. Questions relating to the command of such forces shall be worked out subsequently.

4.   The Military Staff Committee, with the authorization of the Security Council and after consultation with appropriate regional agencies, may establish regional sub-committees.

Article 48

1.   The action required to carry out the decisions of the Security Council for the maintenance of international peace and security shall be taken by all the Members of the United Nations or by some of them, as the Security Council may determine.

2.   Such decisions shall be carried out by the Members of the United Nations directly and through their action in the appropriate international agencies of which they are members.

Article 49

The Members of the United Nations shall join in affording mutual assistance in carrying out the measures decided upon by the Security Council.

Article 50

If preventive or enforcement measures against any state are taken by the Security Council, any other state, whether a Member of the United Nations or not, which finds itself confronted with special economic problems arising from the carrying out of those measures shall have the right to consult the Security Council with regard to a solution of those problems.

Article 51

Nothing in the present Charter shall impair the inherent right of individual or collective self-defence if an armed attack occurs against a Member of the United Nations, until the Security Council has taken measures necessary to maintain international peace and security. Measures taken by Members in the exercise of this right of self-defence shall be immediately reported to the Security Council and shall not in any way affect the authority and responsibility of the Security Council under the present Charter to take at any time such action as it deems necessary in order to maintain or restore international peace and security.

CHAPTER VIII

REGIONAL ARRANGEMENTS

Article 52

1.   Nothing in the present Charter precludes the existence of regional arrangements or agencies for dealing with such matters relating to the maintenance of international peace and security as are appropriate for regional action, provided that such arrangements or agencies and their activities are consistent with the Purposes and Principles of the United Nations.

2.   The Members of the United Nations entering into such arrangements or constituting such agencies shall make every effort to achieve pacific settlement of local disputes through such regional arrangements or by such regional agencies before referring them to the Security Council.

3.   The Security Council shall encourage the development of pacific settlement of local disputes through such regional arrangements or by such regional agencies either on the initiative of the states concerned or by reference from the Security Council.

4.   This Article in no way impairs the application of Articles 34 and 35.

Article 53

1.   The Security Council shall, where appropriate, utilize such regional arrangements or agencies for enforcement action under its authority. But no enforcement action shall be taken under regional arrangements or by regional agencies without the authorization of the Security Council, with the exception of measures against any enemy state, as defined in paragraph 2 of this Article, provided for pursuant to Article 107 or in regional arrangements directed against renewal of aggressive policy on the part of any such state, until such time as the Organization may, on request of the Governments concerned, be charged with the responsibility for preventing further aggression by such a state.

2.   The term enemy state as used in paragraph 1 of this Article applies to any state which during the Second World War has been an enemy of any signatory of the present Charter.

Article 54

The Security Council shall at all times be kept fully informed of activities undertaken or in contemplation under regional arrangements or by regional agencies for the maintenance of international peace and security.

CHAPTER IX

INTERNATIONAL ECONOMIC AND SOCIAL CO-OPERATION

Article 55

With a view to the creation of conditions of stability and well-being which are necessary for peaceful and friendly relations among nations based on respect for the principle of equal rights and self-determination of peoples, the United Nations shall promote:

a. higher standards of living, full employment, and conditions of economic and social progress and development;

b. solutions of international economic, social, health, and related problems; and international cultural and educational co-operation; and

c. universal respect for, and observance of, human rights and fundamental freedoms for all without distinction as to race, sex, language, or religion.

Article 56

All Members pledge themselves to take joint and separate action in co-operation with the Organization for the achievement of the purposes set forth in Article 55.

Article 57

1. The various specialized agencies, established by intergovernmental agreement and having wide international responsibilities, as defined in their basic instruments, in economic, social, cultural, educational, health, and related fields, shall be brought into relationship with the United Nations in accordance with the provisions of Article 63.

2. Such agencies thus brought into relationship with the United Nations are hereinafter referred to as specialized agencies.

Article 58

The Organization shall make recommendations for the co-ordination of the policies and activities of the specialized agencies.

Article 59

The Organization shall, where appropriate, initiate negotiations among the states concerned for the creation of any new specialized agencies required for the accomplishment of the purposes set forth in Article 55.

Article 60

Responsibility for the discharge of the functions of the Organization set forth in this Chapter shall be vested in the General Assembly and, under the authority of the General Assembly, in the Economic and Social Council, which shall have for this purpose the powers set forth in Chapter X.

CHAPTER X

THE ECONOMIC AND SOCIAL COUNCIL

Composition

Article 61

1. The Economic and Social Council shall consist of fifty-four Members of the United Nations elected by the General Assembly.

2. Subject to the provisions of paragraph 3, eighteen members of the Economic and Social Council shall be elected each year for a term of three years. A retiring member shall be eligible for immediate re-election.

3. At the first election after the increase in the membership of the Economic and Social Council from twenty-seven to fifty-four members, in addition to the members elected in place of the nine members whose term of office expires at the end of that year, twenty-seven additional members shall be elected. Of these twenty-seven additional members, the term of office of nine members so elected shall expire at the end of one year, and of nine other members at the end of two years, in accordance with arrangements made by the General Assembly.

4. Each member of the Economic and Social Council shall have one representative.

Functions and Powers

Article 62

1. The Economic and Social Council may make or initiate studies and reports with respect to international economic, social, cultural, educational, health, and related matters and may make recommendations with respect to any such matters to the General Assembly to the Members of the United Nations, and to the specialized agencies concerned.

2. It may make recommendations for the purpose of promoting respect for, and observance of, human rights and fundamental freedoms for all.

3. It may prepare draft conventions for submission to the General Assembly, with respect to matters falling within its competence.

4. It may call, in accordance with the rules prescribed by the United Nations, international conferences on matters falling within its competence.

Article 63

1. The Economic and Social Council may enter into agreements with any of the agencies referred to in Article 57, defining the terms on which the agency concerned shall be brought into relationship with the United Nations. Such agreements shall be subject to approval by the General Assembly.

2. It may co-ordinate the activities of the specialized agencies through consultation with and recommendations to such agencies and through recommendations to the General Assembly and to the Members of the United Nations.

Article 64

1. The Economic and Social Council may take appropriate steps to obtain regular reports from the specialized agencies. It may make arrangements with the Members of the United Nations and with the specialized agencies to obtain reports on the steps taken to give effect to its own recommendations and to recommendations on matters falling within its competence made by the General Assembly.

2. It may communicate its observations on these reports to the General Assembly.

Article 65

The Economic and Social Council may furnish information to the Security Council and shall assist the Security Council upon its request.

Article 66

1. The Economic and Social Council shall perform such functions as fall within its competence in connection with the carrying out of the recommendations of the General Assembly.

2.   It may, with the approval of the General Assembly, perform services at the request of Members of the United Nations and at the request of specialized agencies.

3.   It shall perform such other functions as are specified elsewhere in the present Charter or as may be assigned to it by the General Assembly.

Voting

Article 67

1.   Each member of the Economic and Social Council shall have one vote.

2.   Decisions of the Economic and Social Council shall be made by a majority of the members present and voting.

Procedure

Article 68

The Economic and Social Council shall set up commissions in economic and social fields and for the promotion of human rights, and such other commissions as may be required for the performance of its functions.

Article 69

The Economic and Social Council shall invite any Member of the United Nations to participate, without vote, in its deliberations on any matter of particular concern to that Member.

Article 70

The Economic and Social Council may make arrangements for representatives of the specialized agencies to participate, without vote, in its deliberations and in those of the commissions established by it, and for its representatives to participate in the deliberations of the specialized agencies.

Article 71

The Economic and Social Council may make suitable arrangements for consultation with non-governmental organizations which are concerned with matters within its competence. Such arrangements may be made with international organizations and, where appropriate, with national organizations after consultation with the Member of the United Nations concerned.

Article 72

1.   The Economic and Social Council shall adopt its own rules of procedure, including the method of selecting its President.

2.   The Economic and Social Council shall meet as required in accordance with its rules, which shall include provision for the convening of meetings on the request of a majority of its members.

CHAPTER XI

DECLARATION REGARDING NON-SELF-GOVERNING TERRITORIES

Article 73

Members of the United Nations which have or assume responsibilities for the administration of territories whose peoples have not yet attained a full measure of self-government recognize the principle that the interests of the inhabitants of these territories are paramount, and accept as a sacred trust the obligation to promote to the utmost, within the system of international peace and security established by the present Charter, the well-being of the inhabitants of these territories, and, to this end:

a. to ensure, with due respect for the culture of the peoples concerned, their political, economic, social, and educational advancement, their just treatment, and their protection against abuses;

b. to develop self-government, to take due account of the political aspirations of the peoples, and to assist them in the progressive development of their free political institutions, according to the particular circumstances of each territory and its peoples and their varying stages of advancement;

c. to further international peace and security;

d. to promote constructive measures of development, to encourage research, and to co-operate with one another and, when and where appropriate, with specialized international bodies with a view to the practical achievement of the social, economic, and scientific purposes set forth in this Article; and

e. to transmit regularly to the Secretary-General for information purposes, subject to such limitation as security and constitutional considerations may require, statistical and other information of a technical nature relating to economic, social, and educational conditions in the territories for which they are respectively responsible other than those territories to which Chapters XII and XIII apply.

Article 74

Members of the United Nations also agree that their policy in respect of the territories to which this Chapter applies, no less than in respect of their metropolitan areas, must be based on the general principle of good-neighbourliness, due account being taken of the interests and well-being of the rest of the world, in social, economic, and commercial matters,

CHAPTER XII

INTERNATIONAL TRUSTEESHIP SYSTEM

Article 75

The United Nations shall establish under its authority an international trusteeship system for the administration and supervision of such territories as may be placed there-under by subsequent individual agreements. These territories are hereinafter referred to as trust territories.

Article 76

The basic objectives of the trusteeship system, in accordance with the Purposes of the United Nations laid down in Article 1 of the present Charter, shall be:

a. to further international peace and security;

b. to promote the political, economic, social, and educational advancement of the inhabitants of the trust territories, and their progressive development towards self-government or independence as may be appropriate to the particular circumstances of each territory and its peoples and the freely expressed wishes of the peoples concerned, and as may be provided by the terms of each trusteeship agreement;

c. to encourage respect for human rights and for fundamental freedoms for all without distinction as to race, sex, language, or religion, and to encourage recognition of the interdependence of the peoples of the world; and

d.   to ensure equal treatment in social, economic, and commercial matters for all Members of the United Nations and their nationals, and also equal treatment for the latter in the administration of justice, without prejudice to the attainment of the foregoing objectives and subject to the provisions of Article 80.

Article 77

1.   The trusteeship system shall apply to such territories in the following categories as may be placed thereunder by means of trusteeship agreements:

a.   territories now held under mandate;

b.   territories which may be detached from enemy states as a result of the Second World War; and

c.   territories voluntarily placed under the system by states responsible for their administration.

2.   It will be a matter for subsequent agreement as to which territories in the foregoing categories will be brought under the trusteeship system and upon what terms.

Article 78

The trusteeship system shall not apply to territories which have become Members of the United Nations, relationship among which shall be based on respect for the principle of sovereign equality.

Article 79

The terms of trusteeship for each territory to be placed under the trusteeship system, including any alteration or amendment, shall be agreed upon by the states directly concerned, including the mandatory power in the case of territories held under mandate by a Member of the United Nations, and shall be approved as provided for in Articles 83 and 85.

Article 80

1.   Except as may be agreed upon in individual trusteeship agreements, made under Articles 77, 79, and 81, placing each territory under the trusteeship system, and until such agreements have been concluded, nothing in this Chapter shall be construed in or of itself to alter in any manner the rights whatsoever of any states or any peoples or the terms of existing international instruments to which Members of the United Nations may respectively be parties.

2.   Paragraph 1 of this Article shall not be interpreted as giving grounds for delay or postponement of the negotiation and conclusion of agreements for placing mandated and other territories under the trusteeship system as provided for in Article 77.

Article 81

The trusteeship agreement shall in each case include the terms under which the trust territory will be administered and designate the authority which will exercise the administration of the trust territory. Such authority, hereinafter called the administering authority, may be one or more states or the Organization itself.

Article 82

There may be designated, in any trusteeship agreement, a strategic area or areas which may include part or all of the trust territory to which the agreement applies, without prejudice to any special agreement or agreements made under Article 43.

Article 83

1.   All functions of the United Nations relating to strategic areas, including the approval of the terms of the trusteeship agreements and of their alteration or amendment, shall be exercised by the Security Council.

2.   The basic objectives set forth in Article 76 shall be applicable to the people of each strategic area.

3.   The Security Council shall, subject to the provisions of the trusteeship agreements and without prejudice to security considerations, avail itself of the assistance of the Trusteeship Council to perform those functions of the United Nations under the trusteeship system relating to political, economic, social, and educational matters in the strategic areas.

Article 84

It shall be the duty of the administering authority to ensure that the trust territory shall play its part in the maintenance of international peace and security. To this end the administering authority may make use of volunteer forces, facilities, and assistance from the trust territory in carrying out the obligations towards the Security Council undertaken in this regard by the administering authority, as well as for local defence and the maintenance of law and order within the trust territory.

Article 85

1.   The functions of the United Nations with regard to trusteeship agreements for all areas not designated as strategic, including the approval of the terms of the trusteeship agreements and of their alteration or amendment, shall be exercised by the General Assembly.

2.   The Trusteeship Council, operating under the authority of the General Assembly, shall assist the General Assembly in carrying out these functions.

CHAPTER XIII

THE TRUSTEESHIP COUNCIL

Composition

Article 86

1.   The Trusteeship Council shall consist of the following Members of the United Nations:

a.   those Members administering trust territories;

b.   such of those Members mentioned by name in Article 23 as are not administering trust territories; and

c.   as many other Members elected for three-year terms by the General Assembly as may be necessary to ensure that the total number of members of the Trusteeship Council is equally divided between those Members of the United Nations which administer trust territories and those which do not.

2.   Each member of the Trusteeship Council shall designate one specially qualified person to represent it therein.

Functions and Power

Article 87

The General Assembly and, under its authority, the Trusteeship Council, in carrying out their functions, may:

a.   consider reports submitted by the administering authority;

b.   accept petitions and examine them in consultation with the administering authority;

c.   provide for periodic visits to the respective trust territories at times agreed upon with the administering authority; and

d.   take these and other actions in conformity with the terms of the trusteeship agreements.

Article 88

The Trusteeship Council shall formulate a questionnaire on the political, economic, social, and educational advancement of the inhabitants of each trust territory, and the administering authority for each trust territory within the competence of the General Assembly shall make an annual report to the General Assembly upon the basis of such questionnaire.

Voting

Article 89

1.   Each member of the Trusteeship Council shall have one vote.

2.   Decisions of the Trusteeship Council shall be made by a majority of the members present and voting.

Procedure

Article 90

1.   The Trusteeship Council shall adopt its own rules of procedure, including the method of selecting its President.

2.   The Trusteeship Council shall meet as required in accordance with its rules, which shall include provision for the convening of meetings on the request of a majority of its members.

Article 91

The Trusteeship Council shall, when appropriate, avail itself of the assistance of the Economic and Social Council and of the specialized agencies in regard to matters with which they are respectively concerned.

CHAPTER XIV

THE INTERNATIONAL COURT OF JUSTICE

Article 92

The International Court of Justice shall be the principal judicial organ of the United Nations. It shall function in accordance with the annexed Statute, which is based upon the Statute of the Permanent Court of International Justice and forms an integral part of the present Charter.

Article 93

1.   All Members of the United Nations are ipso facto parties to the Statute of the International Court of Justice.

2.   A state which is not a Member of the United Nations may become a party to the Statute of the International Court of Justice on conditions to be determined in each case by the General Assembly upon the recommendation of the Security Council.

Article 94

1.   Each Member of the United Nations undertakes to comply with the decision of the International Court of Justice in any case to which it is a party.

2.   If any party to a case fails to perform the obligations incumbent upon it under a judgment rendered by the Court, the other party may have recourse to the Security

Council, which may, if it deems necessary, make recommendations or decide upon measures to be taken to give effect to the judgment.

Article 95

Nothing in the present Charter shall prevent Members of the United Nations from entrusting the solution of their differences to other tribunals by virtue of agreements already in existence or which may be concluded in the future.

Article 96

1. The General Assembly or the Security Council may request the International Court of Justice to give an advisory opinion on any legal question.

2. Other organs of the United Nations and specialized agencies, which may at any time be so authorized by the General Assembly, may also request advisory opinions of the Court on legal questions arising within the scope of their activities.

CHAPTER XV

THE SECRETARIAT

Article 97

The Secretariat shall comprise a Secretary-General and such staff as the Organization may require. The Secretary-General shall be appointed by the General Assembly upon the recommendation of the Security Council. He shall be the chief administrative officer of the Organization.

Article 98

The Secretary-General shall act in that capacity in all meetings of the General Assembly, of the Security Council, of the Economic and Social Council, and of the Trusteeship Council, and shall perform such other functions as are entrusted to him by these organs. The Secretary-General shall make an annual report to the General Assembly on the work of the Organization.

Article 99

The Secretary-General may bring to the attention of the Security Council any matter which in his opinion may threaten the maintenance of international peace and security.

Article 100

1. In the performance of their duties the Secretary-General and the staff shall not seek or receive instructions from any government or from any other authority external to the Organization. They shall refrain from any action which might reflect on their position as international officials responsible only to the Organization.

2. Each Member of the United Nations undertakes to respect the exclusively international character of the responsibilities of the Secretary-General and the staff and not to seek to influence them in the discharge of their responsibilities.

Article 101

1. The staff shall be appointed by the Secretary-General under regulations established by the General Assembly.

2. Appropriate staffs shall be permanently assigned to the Economic and Social Council, the Trusteeship Council, and, as required, to other organs of the United Nations. These staffs shall form a part of the Secretariat.

3. The paramount consideration in the employment of the staff and in the determi-

nation of the conditions of service shall be the necessity of securing the highest standards of efficiency, competence, and integrity. Due regard shall be paid to the importance of recruiting the staff on as wide a geographical basis as possible.

CHAPTER XVI

MISCELLANEOUS PROVISIONS

Article 102

1.   Every treaty and every international agreement entered into by any Member of the United Nations after the present Charter comes into force shall as soon as possible be registered with the Secretariat and published by it.

2.   No party to any such treaty or international agreement which has not been registered in accordance with the provisions of paragraph 1 of this Article may invoke that treaty or agreement before any organ of the United Nations.

Article 103

In the event of a conflict between the obligations of the Members of the United Nations under the present Charter and their obligations under any other international agreement, their obligations under the present Charter shall prevail.

Article 104

The Organization shall enjoy in the territory of each of its Members such legal capacity as may be necessary for the exercise of its functions and the fulfilment of its purposes.

Article 105

1.   The Organization shall enjoy in the territory of each of its Members such priv-ileges and immunities as are necessary for the fulfilment of its purposes.

2.   Representatives of the Members of the United Nations and officials of the Organization shall similarly enjoy such privileges and immunities as are necessary for the independent exercise of their functions in connection with the Organization.

3.   The General Assembly may make recommendations with a view to determining the details of the application of paragraphs 1 and 2 of this Article or may propose conventions to the Members of the United Nations for this purpose.

CHAPTER XVII

TRANSITIONAL SECURITY ARRANGEMENTS

Article 106

Pending the coming into force of such special agreements referred to in Article 43 as in the opinion of the Security Council enable it to begin the exercise of its responsibilities under Article 42, the parties to the Four-Nation Declaration, signed at Moscow, 30 October 1943, and France, shall, in accordance with the provisions of paragraph 5 of that Declaration, consult with one another and as occasion requires with other Members of the United Nations with a view to such joint action on behalf of the Organization as may be necessary for the purpose of maintaining international peace and security.

Article 107

Nothing in the present Charter shall invalidate or preclude action, in relation to any state which during the Second World War has been an enemy of any signatory to the present Charter, taken or authorized as a result of that war by the Governments having responsibility for such action.

CHAPTER XVIII

AMENDMENTS

Article 108

Amendments to the present Charter shall come into force for all Members of the United Nations when they have been adopted by a vote of two thirds of the members of the General Assembly and ratified in accordance with their respective constitutional processes by two thirds of the Members of the United Nations, including all the permanent members of the Security Council.

Article 109

1.   A General Conference of the Members of the United Nations for the purpose of reviewing the present Charter may be held at a date and place to be fixed by a two-thirds vote of the members of the General Assembly and by a vote of any nine members of the Security Council. Each Member of the United Nations shall have one vote in the conference.

2.   Any alteration of the present Charter recommended by a two-thirds vote of the conference shall take effect when ratified in accordance with their respective constitutional processes by two thirds of the Members of the United Nations including all the permanent members of the Security Council.

3.   If such a conference has not been held before the tenth annual session of the General Assembly following the coming unto force of the present Charter, the proposal to call such a conference shall be placed on the agenda of that session of the General Assembly, and the conference shall be held if so decided by a majority vote of the members of the General Assembly and by a vote of any seven members of the Security Council.

CHAPTER XIX

RATIFICATION AND SIGNATURE

Article 110

1.   The present Charter shall be ratified by the signatory states in accordance with their respective constitutional processes.

2.   The ratifications shall be deposited with the Government of the United States of America, which shall notify all the signatory states of each deposit as well as the Secretary-General of the Organization when he has been appointed.

3.   The present Charter shall come into force upon the deposit of ratifications by the Republic of China, France, the Union of Soviet Socialist Republics, the United Kingdom of Great Britain and Northern Ireland, and the United States of America, and by a majority of the other signatory states. A protocol of the ratifications deposited shall thereupon be drawn up by the Government of the United States of America which shall communicate copies thereof to all the signatory states.

4.   The states signatory to the present Charter which ratify it after it has come into force will become original Members of the United Nations on the date of the deposit of their respective ratifications.

Article 111

The present Charter, of which the Chinese, French, Russian, English, and Spanish texts are equally authentic, shall remain deposited in the archives of the Government of the United States of America.

Duly certified copies thereof shall be transmitted by that Government to the Governments of the other signatory states.

IN FAITH WHEREOF the representatives of the Governments of the United Nations have signed the present Charter.

DONE at the city of San Francisco the twenty-sixth day of June, one thousand nine hundred and forty-five.

RESOLUTION 866 (1993)

Adopted by the Security Council at its 3281st meeting, on 22 September 1993

The Security Council

Recalling its resolutions 813 (1993) of 26 March 1993 and 856 (1993) of 10 August 1993,

Having considered the report of the Secretary-General (S/26422 and Add.1) dated 9 September 1993 on the proposed establishment of the United Nations Observer Mission in Liberia (UNOMIL),

Noting that the Peace Agreement signed by the three Liberian parties in Cotonou on 25 July 1993 calls on the United Nations and the Military Observer Group (ECOMOG) of the Economic Community of West African States (ECOWAS) to assist in the implementation of the Agreement,

Emphasizing as noted in the Secretary-General's report of 4 August 1993 (S/26200), that the Peace Agreement assigns ECOMOG the primary responsibility of supervising the implementation of the military provisions of the Agreement and envisages that the United Nations role shall be to monitor and verify this process,

Noting that this would be the first peace-keeping mission undertaken by the United Nations in cooperation with a peace-keeping mission already set up by another organization, in this case ECOWAS,

Recognizing that United Nations involvement would contribute significantly to the effective implementation of the Peace Agreement and would serve to underline the international community's commitment to conflict resolution in Liberia,

Commending ECOWAS for its continuing efforts to restore peace, security and stability in Liberia,

Commending also the efforts of the Organization of African Unity in support of the peace process in Liberia,

Stressing the importance of full cooperation and close coordination between UNOMIL and ECOMOG in the implementation of their respective mandates,

Taking note of the deployment of an advance team of United Nations military observers to Liberia as authorized under resolution 856 (1993),

Welcoming the establishment of the Joint Cease-Fire Monitoring Committee (JCMC) composed of the three Liberian parties, ECOMOG and the United Nations,

Welcoming also the formation in Cotonou on 27 August 1993 of the five-member Council of States representing all three Liberian parties, which, in accordance with the Peace Agreement, shall be installed concomitantly with the commencement of the disarmament process and shall be responsible for the day-to-day operation of the transitional government,

Noting that the Peace Agreement calls for legislative and presidential elections to take place approximately seven months after the signing of the Peace Agreement,

1. Welcomes the report of the Secretary-General dated 9 September 1993 (S/26442) on the proposed establishment of UNOMIL;

2. Decides to establish UNOMIL under its authority and under the direction of the Secretary-General through his Special Representative for a period of seven months, subject to the proviso that it will continue beyond 16 December 1993 only upon a review by the Council based on a report from the Secretary-General on whether or not substantive progress has been made towards the implementation of the Peace Agreement and other measures aimed at establishing a lasting peace;

3. Decides that UNOMIL shall compromise military observers as well as medical, engineering, communications, transportation and electoral components, in the numbers indicated in the Secretary-General's report, together with minimal staff necessary to support it, and shall have the following mandate:

    a. To receive and investigate all reports on alleged incidents of violations of the cease-fire agreement and, if the violation cannot be corrected, to report its findings to the Violations Committee established pursuant to the Peace Agreement and to the Secretary-General;

    b. To monitor compliance with other elements of the Peace Agreement, including at points on Liberia's borders with Sierra Leone and other neighbouring countries, and to verify its impartial application, and in particular to assist in the monitoring of compliance with the embargo on delivery of arms and military equipment to Liberia and the cantonment, disarmament and demobilization of combatants;

    c. To observe and verify the election process, including the legislative and presidential elections to be held in accordance with the provisions of the Peace Agreement;

    d. To assist, as appropriate, in the coordination of humanitarian assistance activities in the field in conjunction with the existing United Nations humanitarian relief operation;

    e. To develop a plan and assess financial requirements for the demobilization of combatants;

f. To report on any major violations of international humanitarian law to the Secretary-General;

g. To train ECOMOG engineers in mine clearance and, in cooperation with ECOMOG, coordinate the identification of mines and assist in the clearance of mines and unexploded bombs;

h. Without participation in enforcement operations, to coordinate with ECOMOG in the discharge of ECOMOG's separate responsibilities both formally, through the Violations Committee, and informally;

4. Welcomes the Secretary-General's intention to conclude with the Chairman of ECOWAS an agreement defining, before deployment of UNOMIL, the roles and responsibilities of UNOMIL and ECOWAS in the implementation of the Peace Agreement, in accordance with the concept of operations outlined in Chapter IV of the Secretary-General's report (S/26422), and requests the Secretary-General to keep the Council informed on the progress and outcome of the negotiations leading thereto;

5. Encourages African States to provide the additional troops requested from them by ECOWAS for ECOMOG;

6. Welcomes the steps taken by the Secretary-General to establish a Trust Fund, which would facilitate the sending of reinforcements by African States to ECOMOG, assist in supporting troops of participating ECOMOG countries and also assist in mine-clearing, humanitarian and development activities, as well as the electoral process, and calls on Member States to support the peace process in Liberia by contributing to the Trust Fund;

7. Urges the Liberian parties to commence the encampment, disarmament and demobilization process without delay;

8. Welcomes the decision to establish the transitional government and urges also the Liberian parties to begin the exercise of that government's responsibilities concomitantly with the process described in paragraph 7 above and consistent with the Peace Agreement;

9. Calls on the transitional government to conclude expeditiously, and no later than 60 days after its installation, a Status of Mission Agreement with the United Nations to facilitate the full deployment of UNOMIL;

10. Urges the Liberian parties to finalize the composition of the Elections Commission so that it can promptly undertake the necessary preparation for legislative and presidential elections by March 1994, at the latest, in accordance with the timetable foreseen in the Peace Agreement;

11. Calls on the Liberian parties to cooperate fully in the safe delivery of humanitarian assistance to all parts of the country by the most direct routes, in accordance with the Peace Agreement;

12. Welcomes ECOMOG's stated commitment to ensure the safety of UNOMIL observers and civilian staff and urges the Liberian parties to take all necessary measures to ensure the security and safety of UNOMIL personnel, as well as of the personnel involved in relief operations, and strictly to abide by applicable rules of international humanitarian law;

13. Requests the Secretary-General to submit progress reports to the Council on the implementation of the present resolution by 16 December 1993 and by 16 February 1994;

14. Decides to remain actively seized of the matter.

GLOSSARY

COMBAT SERVICE SUPPORT (CSS)
The support provided to combat forces, primarily in the fields of administration and logistics. [AFM Vol 1 Part 6]

CONFLICT RESOLUTION
The resolution of conflict by conciliation.

[ADP Operations]

CONFLICT TERMINATION
The termination of conflict by force, usually in conjunction with other coercive instruments of policy available to governments - thus transforming the conflict into war.

[ADP Operations]

END STATE
A set of required conditions which, when achieved, result in attainment of the strategic aims set for the campaign. [FM 100-5 Prelim Draft]

ENFORCE
Urge, press home, (argument, demand); impose (action, conduct, upon person etc); compel observance of (law etc). [Concise Oxford Dictionary]

HUMANITARIAN AID
Missions conducted to relieve human suffering, especially in circumstances where responsible authorities in the area are unable, or possibly unwilling, to provide adequate service support to the population. Humanitarian aid missions may be conducted in the context of a peace support operation, or as a completely independent task.

[MC 327, not endorsed]

INTERVENE
Come in as something extraneous; occur in the meantime; (of person or thing) come between, interfere, so as to prevent or modify result etc.

[Concise Oxford Dictionary]

LOGISTICS
The support provided to combat forces, primarily in the fields of administration and logistics. [AFM Vol 1 Part 6]

MINIMUM NECESSARY FORCE
The measured application of violence or coercion, sufficient only to achieve a specific end, demonstrably reasonable, proportionate and appropriate; and confined in effect to the specific and legitimate target intended.

[AFM Wider Peacekeeping]

PEACE
A condition that exists in the relations between groups, classes or states when there is an absence of violence (direct or indirect) or the threat of violence.

[International Peace Academy (New York)]

PEACE BUILDING
Social change that actively seeks to eliminate the likelihood of direct and/or indirect violence.

[International Peace Academy (New York)]

Action to identify and support structures which will tend to strengthen and solidify peace in order to avoid a relapse into conflict.

[UN Report: "An Agenda for Peace"]

Post-conflict diplomatic and military actions which seek to rebuild the institutions and infrastructures of a nation torn by civil war; or build bonds of peaceful mutual benefit among nations formerly at war, in order to avoid a relapse into conflict.

[US Joint Staff]

Post-conflict action to identify and support structures which will tend to strengthen and solidify a political settlement in order to avoid a return to conflict. It includes mechanisms to identify and support structures which will tend to consolidate peace, advance a sense of confidence and well-being and support economic reconstruction, and may require military as well as civilian involvement.   [MC 327, not endorsed]

PEACE ENFORCEMENT
Operations carried out to restore peace between belligerents who do not all consent to intervention and who may be engaged in combat activities.

[ADP Operations]

Military operations in support of diplomatic efforts to restore peace between belligerents who may not be consenting to intervention and who may be engaged in combat activities.

[US Jt Pub 3-07.3]

Military operations (including possible combat actions) in support of diplomatic efforts to restore peace between belligerents who may not be consenting to intervention, and who may be engaged in combat activities.   [US Joint Staff]

Collective security action by air, sea or land forces as may be necessary to maintain or restore international peace and security.

[Based on UN Charter Chapter VII]

Action under Chapter VII of the UN Charter using military means to restore peace in an area of conflict. This can include dealing with an inter-State conflict or with internal conflict to meet a humanitarian need or where state institutions have largely collapsed.

[MC 327, not endorsed]]

A form of armed intervention, or the threat of armed intervention, that is pursuant to international license authorizing the coercive use of military force to compel compliance with internationally expected patterns of behaviour, sanctions or resolutions - the primary purpose of which is the maintenance or restoration of peace under conditions broadly accepted by the international community.   [US term (Apr 93)]

Military operations using appropriate force to separate belligerents, with or without their consent, at any time after a dispute has erupted and prior to a peaceful settlement.

[US Army-Air Force Center for LIC]

PEACEKEEPING
Operations carried out with the consent of the belligerent parties in support of efforts to achieve or maintain peace in order to promote security and sustain life in areas of potential or actual conflict.

[ADP Operations]

Military operations in support of diplomatic efforts to achieve or maintain peace between consenting belligerent parties in areas of potential or actual conflict.

[Composite from US Joint Publication 3-07]

The prevention, containment, moderation and termination of hostilities between or within states, through the medium of a peaceful third party intervention organized and directed internationally using multinational forces of soldiers, police and civilians to restore and maintain peace.   [International Peace Academy
(New York)]

The containment, moderation and/or termination of hostilities between or within states, through the medium of an impartial third party intervention organized and directed internationally; using military forces, and civilians to complement the political process of conflict resolution and to restore and maintain peace.

[MC 327, not endorsed]

Operations in support of efforts to achieve or maintain peace between consenting adversaries in areas of potential or actual conflict, often including but not limited to the use of military personnel or capabilities.   [US Sinai Field Mission (estb 1976)]

The deployment of a UN presence in the field, hitherto with the consent of all the parties concerned, normally involving UN military and/or police personnel and frequently civilians as well. Peace- keeping is a technique that expands the possibilities for both the prevention of conflict and the making of peace.

[UN Report: "An Agenda for Peace"]

Operations conducted with the consent of the belligerent parties, designed to maintain a negotiated truce and help promote conditions which support diplomatic efforts to establish a long-term peace in areas of conflict.   [US Joint Staff]

An operation involving military personnel, but without enforcement powers, established by the United Nations to help maintain or restore peace in areas of conflict.
["The Blue Helmets"]

Non-combat military operations (exclusive of self-defence actions), that are undertaken by outside forces with the consent of all major belligerent parties, designed to monitor and facilitate implementation of an existing truce agreement in support of diplomatic efforts to reach a comprehensive peace settlement.
[US term (Apr 93)]

Operations, conducted with the consent of the belligerent parties, designed to maintain a negotiated truce and help promote conditions that support the diplomatic efforts to establish a long-term peace in areas of conflict. (May also be called trucekeeping.)
[US Joint Pub 3-07.3]

Operations conducted impartially, with the consent of all the belligerents, to maintain a negotiated truce while diplomatic efforts continue to achieve a peaceful settlement. (May also be called truce-keeping.)
[US Army-Air Force Center for LIC]

PEACEKEEPING OPERATIONS
Military operations conducted with the consent of the belligerent parties to a conflict to maintain a negotiated truce in support of diplomatic efforts to achieve or maintain peace. Peacekeeping operations will be undertaken in response to a request from the host nation(s) to an international organization or to friendly nation(s).
[US manual: 'Peacekeeping Operations']

Operations aiming to prevent conflict, or its resumption, by the physical separation of hostile elements by a third party to allow negotiations to reach a political settlement.
[AFM Vol V Part 1]

PEACEMAKING
Efforts to settle a conflict or maintain peace, preferably through diplomacy, persuasion, mediation, negotiation or other forms of peaceful settlement; but sometimes requiring the use of military force or other means of coercion.
[US manual: 'Peacekeeping Operations']

Efforts to settle a conflict through mediation, negotiation or other forms of peaceful settlement. [Peacemaking constitutes the overall environment within which peacekeeping and peace enforcement operate. It precedes the initiation of military operations and continues throughout and even after their execution.]

[International Peace Academy
(Peacekeeper's Handbook)]

Action to bring hostile parties to agreement, essentially through such peaceful means as those foreseen in Chapter VI of the UN Charter. UN

[Report: "An Agenda for Peace"]

Diplomatic actions conducted after the commencement of conflict, with the aim of establishing a peaceful settlement. They can include the provision of good offices, mediation, conciliation and such actions as diplomatic isolation and sanctions.

[MC 327, not endorsed]

Diplomatic actions to achieve a negotiated truce resulting in a peaceful settlement with an atmosphere of trust, peace, and cooperation among all belligerent parties. These actions may be taken at any time before or after a dispute has erupted.

[US Army-Air Force Center for
LIC]

PEACE SUPPORT OPERATIONS

The generic term encompassing peacekeeping, Wider Peacekeeping and peace enforcement. [ADP Operations]

The umbrella term encompassing diplomatic actions (peacemaking), traditional peacekeeping (sometimes referred to as truce-keeping), and forceful military actions (peace-enforcement), to obtain peace.

[US Army-Air Force Center for
LIC]

PREVENTIVE DIPLOMACY

Action to prevent disputes from arising between parties, to prevent existing disputes from escalating into conflicts and to limit the spread of the latter when they occur.

[UN Report: "An Agenda for
Peace" and MC 327]

Diplomatic action in advance of predictable crises aimed at resolving sources of conflict before violence breaks out, and to limit the spread of conflict if it erupts.

[US Joint Staff]

WIDER PEACEKEEPING

The wider aspects of peacekeeping operations carried out with the consent of the belligerent parties but in an environment that may be highly volatile.

[ADP Operations]

HISTORICAL
SUPPLEMENT

ONUMOZ

ONUMOZ

BACKGROUND

Until 1974 Mozambique was a Portuguese colony which, from 1964, had been involved in a guerrilla war waged by the Mozambique Liberation Front (Frelimo). Following the change of government in Portugal in 1974, Mozambique was granted independence in 1975. The accession to power in Mozambique of Frelimo led to armed resistance by groups opposed to Frelimo's Marxist-Leninist policies. The armed opposition centred on the Mozambique National Resistance (Renamo) initially supported by the Smith regime in Rhodesia and subsequently through the 1980s it was supported by South Africa. Eventually in 1989 a number of mediation and peace efforts were made which in 1990 saw contact between the two sides and this eventually led to further direct talks in Rome in 1991 resulting in a cease-fire agreement signed in August 1992.

These 14 years of civil war had wrecked much of the country's communications system and infrastructure, Mozambique had in addition suffered for decades from serious drought conditions so that food was in short supply. Several millions of Mozambicans were internally displaced or were refugees in neighbouring countries. Further the abundance of arms resulted in many armed bandits operating outside the control of the armed forces of either side.

CREATION OF ONUMOZ

The signing of a general peace agreement between the Government of the Republic of Mozambique and the Mozambique National Resistance (RENAMO) resulted in the UN Security-Council passing Resolution 782 on 13 October 1992 which approved the appointment by the UN Secretary-General of an interim Special Representative and the despatch to Mozambique of a team of up to 25 military observers. In addition the subsequent establishment of a UN operation in Mozambique and particularly its cost, were also to be considered.

The 21 military observers despatched were drawn from existing peace-keeping missions and arrived in Mozambique on 21 October 1992. Logistic difficulties and disputes between the two sides, including some military operations, delayed progress towards the establishment of the machinery for the monitoring and verification of the cease-fire. However after strenuous efforts by the UN Special Representative, it was possible to establish the Commissions foreseen in the peace agreement: the overall Supervisory & Monitoring Commission, and its subsidiaries, the Cease-Fire Commission, the Reintegration Commission and the Joint Commission for the Formation of the Mozambican Defence Forces. The members for these Commissions came from a number of states with, in some cases, a UN chairman.

The UN Secretary-General reported that a mandate for a UN operation would seek to cover four areas: Political to facilitate implementation of the cease-fire by chairing the Supervisory & Monitoring Commission and subordinate commissions. Military monitoring the cease-fire, the separation and concentration of forces, demobilization and collection, storage and destruction of weapons. Monitoring and verifying the withdrawal of foreign troops and the disbanding of private and irregular armed groups. Authorizing security for vital infrastructure and providing security for UN and international activities in support of the peace process. Electoral to provide technical assistance and monitor the electoral process. Humanitarian to co-ordinate and monitor all humanitarian assistance operations, in particular those concerned with refugees, demilitarized military and other local populations: there were some 1.5 million refugees in neighbouring countries. A further related task would be the mine-awareness and mine-clearing programme. There were estimated to be some 2 million mines in Mozambique, some dating back to the colonial era!

It was envisaged that ONUMOZ would primarily operate through teams of military observers at the 49 locations designated as 'assembly areas' in 3 military regions, and elsewhere in the field. They would work with, but be separate from, the monitoring groups from the two parties also based at each location. Teams would also be deployed at airports, ports and other critical areas including RENAMO HQ. Although some observers would be collocated with armed UN troops, their security was primarily the responsibility of the parties that controlled the zone in which they were based.

The soldiers from the two parties to be assembled and demilitarized - envisaged as some 110,000 strong - would need food and other supplies and an ONUMOZ technical unit would work with the UN office co-ordinating humanitarian assistance (UNOHAC). Given the need to withdraw all foreign troops, in order to secure the 'corridors' for the movement of humanitarian aid, ONUMOZ would have to undertake this task which would require 5 self-sufficient infantry battalions plus three self-sufficient engineer companies with mine-clearance and road repair capability. In addition an HQ company plus communications, aviation units with up to 24 aircraft (rotary & fixed wing) and also medical and logistics support would be required.

In addition some 150 international electoral officers and support staff were required to initiate the electoral component, supplemented later by up to 1200 international observers of the elections. Finally a body of professional international support staff and UN volunteers for administrative tasks were also required.

Subsequent to the Report of the UN Secretary-General to the Security Council in December 1992, the passage of Resolution 797 of 16 December 1992 established a United Nations Operation in Mozambique (ONUMOZ) along the lines envisaged by the Secretary-General in his earlier report.

Internal Mozambican concerns over the presence of foreign troops and over the origins of some of the contributing countries delayed the deployment of ONUMOZ, as did administration within donor countries and delays in obtaining suitable equipment. Within Mozambique itself, an early problem adversely affecting ONUMOZ operations was the need to provide advance information of all UN military personnel movement which reflected the continued deep mistrust between the two opposing sides characterised by their reluctance to begin the assembly and demilitarization process until certain that ONUMOZ was fully deployed and that the opposing group's forces were clearly being subject to cantonment and demilitarization.

Nevertheless as a result of efforts by the Force Commander after his arrival in mid-February 1993 and the growing ONUMOZ presence in the succeeding months, the withdrawal of foreign troops from the vital communications corridors in Mozambique was completed by early June and a few of the assembly areas for cantonment and demilitarization had been agreed by both sides and were operational with some 14,000 soldiers having been registered within these.

The difficulties encountered in these early months demonstrated that the timetable envisaged for the work leading up to elections, initially expected in October 1993, was far too ambitious. The effect of the 6 month rainy season on the electoral registration process meant that even if cantonment and demobilisation were speeded up to be completed by early 1994, elections could not now be expected at the best before the autumn of 1994 and perhaps not until the late spring of 1995 after the second rainy season.

By August 1993, deployment of the military component of ONUMOZ - some 6,000 strong - was complete and with regard to the Milobs just over 350 were deployed in the main Headquarters of the two opposing forces, in the assembly areas and conducting investigations into alleged cease-fire violations. In addition work had begun on the formation of a new Mozambique Defence Force under supervision of observers from France, Britain and Portugal, as statutory members of the 'Joint Commission'. 100 officers - 50 from each of the opposing parties - went for training in Zimbabwe in August with a further group of 440 starting training in October. The aim of the programme to train a corps of officers for the new national army, was run by personnel from the United Kingdom. The French and Portuguese training teams had also commenced their training of certain elements of the new force and men from the RENAMO forces were among those being trained at the year's end.

The decline in local violence and feeling of insecurity in the country following the deployment of ONUMOZ, albeit only gradual, did result in some repatriation of refugees with about 20% having returned by August. A key feature in encouraging further repatriations was the start of the cantonment and demobilisation programme demonstrating that peace was a reality.

In the autumn of 1993 the Secretary-General himself visited Mozambique and as a result of his discussions with the two opposing leaders, was able to encourage greater flexibility and willingness over the cantonment and demobilisation phase in order to hasten the peace process. A result of these negotiations led to the agreement to establish assembly areas for one party's forces outside the area directly under its control and also to begin the dismantling of military and para-military groups simultaneously - a previous stumbling block.

Further progress was also made with discussion on the preparations for the elections and certain key administrative joint commissions, as well as the furtherance of UN supervision of all police activities.

On the military side, the formed units carried out extensive patrols by air and land on the main transport corridors as well as manning temporary road checkpoints to monitor traffic. Food convoys for the assembly areas were escorted while in addition to guarding key infrastructure installations such as oil pumping stations, work was carried out in repairing major access routes. However even by November 1993, there was still a high level of armed banditry in one particular province and international humanitarian organisations were reluctant to operate there. The establishment of unarmed Milobs in that part of the country was also difficult.

There was also a clear need for greater security along the main transport corridors and other key routes, as well as more general protection for humanitarian aid convoys. This need caused the Secretary-General to emphasize the necessity to bring the military component of ONUMOZ up to the originally envisaged level of 7,500. Just before the end of the year in response to this both the Australian and New Zealand governments advised the Secretary-General that they would make troops available to ONUMOZ.

Up to November 1993, there had been few reported violations of the cease-fire and the work of ONUMOZ in investigating alleged breaches and establishing clear guidelines to differentiate between military and logistic troop movements were a contributory factor to this. In turn, the quieter overall situation hastened the resettlement of internally displaced persons so that as many as 1.2 million of the estimated 4-5 million had returned to their home areas by the end of the year, while externally based refugee repatriations had climbed to some 400,000.

In addition, the more stable environment created by ONUMOZ's operations enabled the development of proper communications between the government administration and that of RENAMO in areas under the latter's control. This aided both humanitarian work and reintegration of demobilized personnel. Given the clear progress in Mozambique, the mandate of ONUMOZ was extended for a further six month period by Resolution 882(1993) of 5 November 1993.

The long-awaited assembly of troops from both the Government and RENAMO sides began at the end of November 1993 and in January 1994 disarmament of the many para-military forces began. Both operations were supervised by the UN forces with the UN Military Observers playing a major role in the process.

Although there was a significant reduction in the Force's strength as a result of withdrawals of elements of national contingents at the end of their initial tour without their being replaced: which led in particular to a shortage of infantry, the Force still remained viable. Then in late February the Security Council agreed to increase the numbers of UN Civilian Police (UNCIVPOL) allocated to the force as the UNCIVPOL had a key role in helping to stabilize life and to re-establish law and order.

In early May 1994, the Security-Council extended the mandate of ONUMOZ for a further six months to cover the national elections due on 27/28 October 1994. However by July, although there had been considerable progress in some areas, ONUMOZ was con-cerned that the assembling and demobilisation of the troops from both sides was falling well behind the schedule that was required if the process was to be completed before the elections. At that time only 46% of Government forces and 54% of those from RENAMO had been demobilised. Further there were difficulties with the creation of the new Defence Force, only 3,000 had completed their training with a further 1,000 currently undergoing training out of the 30,000 it had been planned to train by October. Shortage of staff from donor countries to train the Defence Force was a factor, but the main problem lay in the local administration of the selection process and the delays had led to unrest among soldiers awaiting training or demobilisation.

In parallel with these tasks, ONUMOZ with help from other countries including the USA, Norway and the UK, was supporting greater de-mining training and clearance tasks. As a result vehicular access was now possible to some areas that had been isolated for many years and a national mine register had been completed.

By late August 1994 thanks to great efforts by all parties, the assembly of troops was substantially completed only a week behind schedule and many weapons had been collected in central holding points. Nevertheless there was still concern over the need to demobilise all the troops before the elections. Linked with this was the on-going problem of the slow formation of the new Defence Force. This was important because not only was the new Force due to take over formal control of various duties from Government forces, but it was also to relieve ONUMOZ of certain key point guard tasks as the UN force was expected to start to withdraw immediately after the election.

However as the planned date for the elections approached, the Secretary-General reported that although there were still unresolved problems with banditry rife in some areas, and progress in extending the control of the police and the new Defence Force was slow, he felt that significant progress had been made. He considered that all the indications were that the necessary conditions would exist in October for free and fair elections to be supervised by international electoral observer teams working alongside ONUMOZ.

SUMMARY

The deployment of ONUMOZ provided both sides in the earlier conflict with the necessary reassurance to go forward with the peace agreement. This in turn allowed the demobilization process to have a realistic prospect of completion with a subsequent general improvement in civilian belief in the stability of the country. In addition this enabled resources to be targeted against the armed banditry still occurring in certain areas.

Therefore while ONUMOZ could not either create or guarantee the security situation within the country, the force had provided an important stabilising element that encouraged the two sides in Mozambique to put into effect the peace-process and the country was now within sight of elections.

ONUMOZ : FACTS

Location: Mozambique

Duration: 9 months initial deployment, extended until end November 1994.

Function: Cease-fire monitoring; disarm and demobilize; humanitarian; election registration and monitoring: rehabilitation of civil administration.

Authorization: Recorded in the following UN Security Council Resolutions:

Resolution No Date	**Resolution**
782 (1992) 13/10/92	Approves SG's appointment of Special Representative to Mozambique and despatch of military observers.
797 (1992) 16/12/92	Establishes UN Operation in Mozambique (ONUMOZ) until 31 October 1992.
818 (1993) 14/4/93	Urges Government of Mozambique and Renamo to comply with terms of Peace Agreement.
850 (1993) 9/7/93	Urges RENAMO and Government of Mozambique to cooperate with ONUMOZ and begin demobilization.
879 (1993) 29/10/93	Extends ONUMOZ until 15 November 1993.
882 (1993) 5/11/93	Welcomes agreement between parties in Mozambique; renews ONUMOZ for six months.
898 (1994) 23/2/94	Increases UNCIVPOL to 1,144 and seeks reassurance as to progress with the peace process.
916 (1994)	Extends ONUMOZ until 15/11/94, in order to cover elections due in late October.

Strength: As at 18/4/94, formed units & HQ staff total 5,914 including some 300 Military Observers.

Contributors: (formed units: *=infantry unit.   Argentina, Australia, Bangladesh*, Botswana*, Brazil*, India, Italy, Japan, New Zealand, Portugal, Uruguay*, Zambia*.

Costs: Estimated for first 18 months - US $535 million. Estimate for 1/5-15/11/94

UNOSOM

UNOSOM

POLITICAL BACKGROUND

The Republic of Somalia came into being as an independent state in 1960 from the junction of the former British Somaliland and the Italian Trusteeship Territory. With a population of some seven million, the Somalis are divided into six major clan groupings and numerous sub-clans which have survived despite a period of a strict dictatorship of Siad Barre between 1969 and 1991.

For much of its recent history the country has been wracked by periodic droughts, crushing poverty and endemic banditry, all made worse by the brief but destructive lost war with Ethiopia in 1977-8. From 1981 Somalia faced civil war with various factions mounting attacks on the government which managed however to cling on until the end of 1990 when the opponents of Barre closed in on the capital Mogadishu. The major factions of the opposition were by 1990 known as: The Somali National Movement (SNM); Somali Salvation Democratic Front (SSDF); United Somali Movement (USC); Somali National Front (SNF) and the Somali Patriotic Movement (SPM). These factions all had at least a few thousand armed supporters with some armoured vehicles, anti-aircraft artillery, mortars and in some instances, even field artillery and rockets.

In mid-January 1991 Barre fled but an attempt by one group to install a provisional government and as President Ali Mahdi, one leader of a faction in the USC, without consulting the other opposition groups led to armed opposition. This opposition was led by General Aideed the leader of another faction of the USC, with support from the SNM and most of the SPM. This meant that no effective central government could be created.

In spite of efforts of the other African countries to broker peace agreements, sporadic armed clashes continued throughout 1991, notably between supporters of General Aideed and the "Interim President", Ali Mahdi. In late November 1991, the inter-faction disputes turned into full-scale fighting in Mogadishu.

Apart from this destructive fighting, the Somali National Movement, primarily based in the northern region, seceded in May 1991 and sought to found an independent Somaliland free from what it perceived as unfair "southern domination".

During 1991 and early 1992 forces loyal to Barre also continue to launch attacks primarily from the south, in attempts to restore him to power. These were unsuccessful and in April 1992 Barre fled to Kenya.

ECONOMIC AND REFUGEE BACKGROUND

After at least fifteen years of war the fragile economy and agricultural capability had been destroyed. Coupled with a decade of famine there were hundreds of thousands of refugees within the country. In 1992 the United Nations' High Commissioner for Refugees estimated that six million Somalis suffered from malnutrition and disease, and that over one and a half million of these were at immediate risk of starvation.

Non-governmental relief agencies had been active in Somalia for several years, many since the 1980's. However, by early 1990 apart from the hazards presented by the many minefields, both in patterned fields around afew important locations, and in numerous scattered route-denial and harrassing fields, relief operations were becoming increasingly crippled by widespread looting and violence fron gunmen - often heavily armed - against both the recipients of relief supplies and on occasion against the agency staff themselves. The control of relief supplies was an important source of economic wealth with the result that perhaps as much as 80% of food brought into Somalia failed to reach its intended beneficiaries because of banditry. In addition, during the inter-factional fighting in late 1991 the international relief agencies began to suffer casualties among its staff.

UN ACTION

On 21 January 1992 the Secretary-General of the United Nations asked the Security Council to consider urgent measures to bring an end to the Somali civil war. The next day Resolution 733 (1992) imposed a total arms embargo on Somalia as a first step in establishing a cease-fire thus aiding the distribution of humanitarian aid and promoting national reconciliation.

On 24 April 1992 the UN Security Council adopted Resolution 751 which requested the Secretary-General to deploy a group of 50 UN Observers to monitor the cease-fire supposedly agreed in Mogadishu in March. In addition the Secretary-General was authorised to deploy UN security personnel to protect its own personnel including humanitarian aid workers.

In June 1992 General Aideed agreed to the presence of UN troops in Mogadishu to guard aid convoys but in early July Aideed's supporters claimed that UN flights are carrying military equipment for the rival Mahdi forces. As a result UN flights to Mogadishu were suspended for some time.

UNOSOM I

The first UN observers arrived in Mogadishu in late July 1992 and the UN Security Council warned that if the warring factions did not co-operate, other measures by the UN to deliver humanitarian aid could not be excluded. Then in mid-August General Aideed agreed to armed UN personnel being deployed to protect its humanitarian food supplies and the UN prepared to despatch some 500 UN troops. Shortly after, on 14 August, the President of the United States of America announced a food airlift to Somalia to be mounted via Kenya and on 28 August the UN passed Resolution 775 which authorised the deployment of some 3,500 UN troops as a protective force for the humanitarian aid. The first of the additional UN armed troops, provided by Pakistan, arrived in Mogadishu in mid-September 1992. They were mandated to use force only in self-defence.

There were continuing problems with armed gangs (often called 'technicals') and looting in Mogadishu, including at the airport - one of the key routes for food supplies. Although in mid-November, after initial disagreements with General Aideed, the UN troops were able to take control of the airport, nevertheless the situation in Mogadishu continued to deteriorate with the gangs making the relief work more and more hazardous.

In November the Secretary-General's new adviser in Somalia prepared a report detailing the difficulties faced by the UN operation. The Security Council considered this report on 25 November and agreed that the methods employed to date had failed to bring the situation under control. It was therefore considered necessary to change the basis of the UN operations by instituting them under Chapter VII of the Charter and to re-examine the basic premises and principles of the operations being conducted.

In response the Secretary-General outlined to the Security Council five options, all geared to the immediate humanitarian issue, but he noted that in addition there was a need to create conditions for the resolution of the country's political problems and to rehabilitate the economy if the relief work was to have any lasting effect.

The options ranged from relying solely on humanitarian teams with no military protection - clearly ineffective and unacceptable - to the deployment of a major force of troops under direct or indirect UN command designed to end the current violence, disarm the irregular troops and gangs, neutralize their heavy weapons and help create a lasting and effective cease-fire.

The Security-Council passed Resolution 794 on 3 December 1992 which authorised future UN operations under Chapter VII and delayed deployment of the remainder of UNOSOM - at that time just 50 UN Military Observers plus the 715 Pakistani troops - until the situation had been re-assessed.

OPERATION 'RESTORE HOPE' : (UNITAF)

The United States authorities had at the same time examined the situation and concluded that major intervention with US support was required if the scale of human disaster in Somalia was to be reduced. Accordingly the USA offered its support to the UN and the US President directed the execution of 'Operation Restore Hope' on 4 December 1992. This was a combined military operation by US forces under UN auspices to secure the major seaports and airports, key installations and food distribution points in Somalia to provide free passage and security for relief supplies.

The US force with a maximum strength of some 28,000 (8,000 based at sea) was to be assisted by a Unified Task Force (UNITAF) with 20 countries committed to providing over 17,000 men.

The operation was seen as having four phases: 1. The securing of the seaport and airport of Mogadishu, then expanding to Baledogle and Baidoa. 2. The deployment of additional US forces to Baidoa and an expanded lodgement area to secure relief centres further to the west. 3. Expand operations to the south to secure the port and airport at Kismayo plus the airport at Nardere and the land route thence to Baidoa. 4. The transfer of humanitarian relief to UN Peace-Keeping Forces.

The US forces began landing on 9 December and within two days the leaders of the two main warring factions - Ali Mahdi and Aideed -met for talks under US auspices. They agreed a cease-fire and general truce and the disarmament of all irregulars and 'technicals'. In the following weeks, the level of violence in Mogadishu dropped and relief distribution both in the city and to major centres elsewhere was far easier and almost free from harassment. Further a meeting was held in neighbouring Ethiopia of 12 Somali political movements who agreed a nationwide cease-fire and a national reconciliation conference for mid-March 1993.

The existing UNOSOM troops were liaising closely with UNITAF headquarters in Mogadishu as well as providing movement control and escorts for UNOSOM food convoys and flights in the city. Thereby, planning for the eventual transfer of tasks from UNITAF to the future UN peace-keeping force UNSOM II, was already in hand. However by early March 1993, although UNITAF had achieved considerable success deploying into an area sub-divided into some nine 'humanitarian relief sectors' covering approximately 40% of the country, outside this area there was still no secure environment. Indeed even within the UNITAF area, although violence levels had dropped and some disarmament had been achieved, there were still sporadic armed attacks and fire even against UNITAF elements while humanitarian aid workers had also been attacked and in some instances killed.

UNOSOM II

The future role of UNOSOM II was under considerable study. Key features in future progress as seen by the UN Representative were the need to disarm more comprehensively the various factions, particularly with regard to heavy weapons, it was felt that the UNITAF operations had only scratched the surface of the problem with regard to these. It was also important for there to be an an expansion of UNITAF forces into the other areas of the country, particularly the north before UN peace-keeping forces could take over. In addition it was considered that some mine clearance operations were essential.

The Secretary-General noted in his 3 March report to the Security Council that given the still tentative security situation, if UNOSOM II was to implement the tasks set out for it: namely the creation of a secure environment for humanitarian aid, it would require enforcement powers under Chapter VII. US opinion was that the new UN force needed a strength and organisation similar to UNITAF because a traditional peace-keeping force lacked the capability to protect humanitarian supplies.

The Secretary-General considered that UNOSOM II would need a whole range of combat capabilities if the Force was to be capable of enforcement tasks. Among these were: indirect fire weapons, anti-armour and airborne fire-support.

The mandate for UNOSOM II was set out by Resolution 814 of 26 March 1993. This noted that the Force would seek to complete through disarmament and reconciliation the task begun by UNITAF. This would include prevention, and if necessary enforcement action against, breaches of the cease-fire; control of heavy weapons until destruction or transfer to a new national Somali Army; maintenance of local security while a new and effective police force was constituted; continuing military operations to secure humanitarian aid personnel, food stocks and their distribution; the creation of a comprehensive de-mining and mine awareness programme; the repatriation of refugees and the re-settlement of displaced persons.

The force strength was set at around 28,000 men, 8,000 of these being for logistical and administrative functions. This force could, it was felt, be smaller than UNITAF because the latter had broken down a lot of armed resistance and organised fighting with heavy weapons had largely ceased. Further it was planned that an improved intelligence gathering capability would warn of potentially violent situations while an auxiliary police force would free troops for more military tasks. In addition a tactical quick-reaction force from US resources would be available to support the UN Force commander. Apart from the US forces remaining in-theatre but not as part of UNOSOM II, most countries with forces in UNITAF declared their willingness to retain these in UNOSOM II. As the Secretary-General noted, UNOSOM II can be seen as the first humanitarian intervention force in UN history.

The formal transfer from UNITAF to UNOSOM II took place on 4 May 1993. The relief sectors were re-organised into four UNOSOM areas of responsibility: Kismayo, Baidoa, Merca-Mogadishu and Belet Weyne-Jalalasi. By the end of July the force had a strength of little over 20,000 troops drawn from 29 countries and planned additional deployments in following months raised the force to nearly 30,000 by the end of October 1993 (see Appendix). In addition there were some 17,700 US troops of the US Joint Task Force in Somalia, not forming part of UNOSOM II and not under UNOSOM operational command. However this force provided the Quick Reaction Force of some 1,350 deployed in support of UNOSOM II.

In the period from May 1993, as UNOSOM sought to organise a multi-national force with elements in some cases reliant on third countries for weapons and equipment, progress in implementing the mandate was slower than desired. This may have emboldened certain hostile elements among the Somali armed factions who were opposed to any reduction of their power that UNOSOM's actions might bring.

As a result UNOSOM found itself faced with inter-clan and factional fighting in several areas, including in Kismayo which saw an attack there in early May repulsed by the Belgian troops of UNOSOM, but particularly in Mogadishu. In the latter area UNOSOM II's efforts to encourage disarmament, particularly of heavy weapons, were resisted and more active patrolling and weapons confiscations including operations against arms depots were undertaken by UNOSOM forces. The need for such efforts were demon-strated by the fact that in eight months UNITAF and UNOSOM II removed and destroyed hundreds of tons of weapons and ammunition, while in March & April alone seizures consisted of over 1100 small arms and a similar number of rocket launchers and mortars; nearly 50 armoured vehicles including tanks and self-propelled artillery; plus more than 400 other artillery pieces.

These efforts took place in a climate of increasing resistance from the USC/SNA faction in south Mogadishu and several incidents occurred which challenged the course of the disarmament and reconciliation programme, as well as increasing instability in south Mogadishu and stimulating factional interests to prepare for a future of renewed fighting.

A clear demonstration of this was the deliberate ambush on 5 June of a force of UNOSOM II soldiers from the Pakistani contingent. This incident left 25 soldiers killed and 40 wounded. As a result of this attack, the Security Council urged member states to contribute on an emergency basis APCs, tanks and attack helicopters to enable UNOSOM II to confront and deter armed attacks.

Then on 12 July the US Quick Reaction Force under UNOSOM II direction conducted an operation against a major USC/SNA command centre in conjunction with UNOSOM II ground forces. After the withdrawal of UNOSOM troops, western journalists on the scene were attacked and four of them murdered. On 8 August, a routine UNOSOM II patrol of four US soldiers were killed by an explosive device attack on their vehicle.

On 5 September a Nigerian infantry company of UNOSOM II, while relieving the Italian contingent in Mogadishu, was attacked by gunmen. Seven Nigerians were killed and ten wouded. On 9 of the same month a Pakistani UNOSOM II force engaged in clearing roadblocks with US support was attacked by approximately 300 armed militiamen. The US Quick Reaction Force assisted the UNOSOM unit and in all one Pakistani was killed and two others as well as three US soldiers were wounded. Then on 15 September two Italian soldiers were killed by snipers.

Finally on 3 October, elements from the US Joint Task Force, led by US Army Rangers, launched an operation in south Mogadishu designed to capture a number of key aides of Aideed who were suspected of complicity in the 5 June ambush as well as subsequent attacks on UN troops. Although the operation suceded in arresting 24 suspects, in fighting two US helicopters were shot down by militiamen and as the Rangers withdrew with their detainees, they came under concentrated fire. Further US forces and UNOSOM II troops participated in the rescue phase. Eighteen US soldiers lost their lives and 75 were wounded. A US helicopter pilot who was captured, was subsequently released on 14 October.

It should be noted that this last operation was not initially a multilateral operation under UN command or authority, but one by US forces under US command acting in support of the UNOSOM II mandate, only with the rescue phase did UNOSOM II become directly involved.

During all these incidents, particularly in those in October, Somali attackers used women and children as cover for their attacks. It was a matter for deep regret that in the ensuing fighting many Somalis lost their lives.

On 9 October the USC/SNA faction declared a unilateral cessation of hostilities against UNOSOM II forces. However these clashes highlighted the difficulties that beset a peace-keeping force, primarily geared to support of humanitarian aid including that from NGOs, which has also to adopt peace-enforcement measures.

The aftermath of the clashes in the autumn led to a reconsideration by several countries of their troops' presence in ONUSOM II and several national contingents were in fact withdrawn by 31 March 1994. Subsequent efforts by the UN to achieve a stable political and security situation, have therefore been made against a backdrop of a future major reduction in UNOSOM II's strength after March 1994.

In the aftermath of this 'cease-fire', while direct armed confrontation between the USC/SNA and UNOSOM were avoided, the whole of Mogadishu remained tense. In addition, the incidence of armed banditry on the streets increased considerably making movement of commercial, UNOSOM personnel and NGO humanitarian supplies increasingly dangerous. There were a number of incidents of armed robbery and attacks on property resulting in casualties to UNOSOM civilians and NGO staff. As a result NGOs were more reluctant to operate in Mogadishu. Indeed travel was possible in many areas only with an armed escort and many areas were wholly out of bounds.

These problems confirmed the earlier belief that general disarmament, not just the removal of heavy weapons, was a precondition for the establishment of a peaceful and secure environment which was necessary to allow progress to be made towards the long term solution of Somalia's problems. However, in spite of the supposed agreement of all Somali parties to the disarmament process, including the use of coercion where necessary by UNOSOM, the deliberate attacks on UNOSOM by one of the parties rendered this course impractical. Subsequently under Resolution 865 (1993) of 22 September 1993, UNOSOM II tried to convince the Somali parties to carry out disarmament on a voluntary basis through the creation of retraining vocational centres to be manned by the Somalis themselves, with initial assistance from UNOSOM and relevant UN agencies. Unfortunately by early January 1994 the signs were that the major Somali factions were actively rearming in anticipation of renewed inter-factional hostilities and were erecting defensive positions within their 'strategic strongholds' in Mogadishu.

The Secretary-General's earlier suggestion that a further brigade was required by UNOSOM II to bring its strength to over 32,000 in order for it to carry out its mandate, was adversely affected by the decision of three countries to withdraw their contingents by the end of December 1993. This, plus the USA's decision to withdraw 1,400 military logistics personnel at the same time, reduced UNOSOM's strength to some 26,000 on 1 January 1994. With the further withdrawals by the USA and four other countries of their forces before the end of March 1994, the Force will have been reduced to some 20,000 although some remaining contributing countries did increase their commitment to help offset the technological losses of the US withdrawal.

FUTURE MANDATE

The Secretary-General considered that by January 1994, UNOSOM II's mandate was far from being accomplished. This could only be completed when a general election had been held followed by the installation of a government with genuine popular support. However the willingness of the international community to support the Somalis to achieve this goal was dependent on action by the Somalis themselves, particularly in ending violence and resolving differences through discussion. UNOSOM was supported by 12 of the 15 Somali groups that signed the March 1993 accord, but progress depended on the willingness of the remaining three groups which form the rival faction, particularly the SNA, to co-operate with UNOSOM II.

Accordingly on the grounds of likely troop strength and continuing opposition from the SNA, the Secretary-General was obliged to recommend the exclusion of disarmament, coercive if necessary, from the future mandate for UNOSOM II. Nor would the Force seek to intervene in any future inter-factional fighting. The emphasis would rest on defending UNOSOM personnel, securing the important ports and essential infrastructure and assist the Somalis with the improvement of the police and judicial systems. As agreed at the recent humanitarian Conference, humanitarian aid would be channelled only to those areas where security existed and appropriate Somali institutions existed.

In the wake of the conflict between the SNA and the forces of UNOSOM II and the USA and the subsequent withdrawals of US and some other forces, in early February the Security Council revised the Mandate along the lines suggested by the Secretary-General.

The emphasis now lay on a more limited role of securing key points such as airports, ports and main routes, for humanitarian aid and protecting these convoys. Further the Force was to be reduced to 22,000 including 2,500 logistic troops, with a view to completing the Force's work by March 1995 by which time elections should have been held, followed by the establishment of a national government.

The new Mandate gave a new impetus to the peace process and steps were taken to normalize the relationship between UNOSOM II and the SNA while maintaining its links with the SSA. However in spite of a new inter-clan peace agreement signed in late March, there was a continuation of the general deterioration of the security situation in certain areas including Mogadishu with inter-clan and inter-factional fighting increasing. All Somali parties were clearly anxious to improve their positions in terms of ground held before the next National Reconciliation Conference initially planned for the spring. Particularly noticeable was the reconstruction and arming of 'technicals' vehicles.

Although fighting has rarely been directed specifically against UNOSOM II forces, there have been UNOSOM casualties and fighting had impeded humanitarian work and indeed aid distribution in Mogadishu was halted for some six weeks in the summer.

The smaller resources of UNOSOM II meant that the area of operation was more restricted and some humanitarian convoys could not therefore always be escorted. However the Force was still providing security for key facilities, particularly in Mogadishu and direct assistance through patrolling on key routes, as well as aiding the reconstitution of the Somali Police Force and the extension of their control.

ACHIEVEMENTS

It would be wrong to allow the difficulties to overshadow completely the many achievements of UNITAF and UNSOM II. The mandate of UNOSOM II called for it to act not only in the political and security fields, but also to seek to assist in the reconstruction of the social, material and economic infrastructure. This latter work covers various aspects and has had many successes.

As a result of UNOSOM II's efforts, over 6,500 policemen are serving at regional and district levels and courts of various types have also been re-established with properly administered prisons. The introduction of a Somali Police Rapid Deployment Force by March 1994 will free UNOSOM II military personnel from this role. In spite of insecurity in some areas which hinders humanitarian aid and resettlement of refugees, there has been considerable progress in this field with a more co-ordinated approach through regular meetings of the various Agencies involved and the transition towards Somali control of these processes is being emphasised. Further in many districts country-wide a number of local councils have been chosen by the Somalis themselves, thus starting the process of rehabilitating the local administrative machinery and aiding resettlement.

In some areas life was returning to normal with an increase in agricultural production and the rebuilding of the judiciary and police system. Further some tens of thousands of displaced persons had been resettled, although several hundreds of thousands still remain displaced. Although de-mining tasks had been adversely affected by the lack of local security which has prevented the introduction of professional assistance from outside Somalia. Efforts were being concentrated on a local 'self-help' scheme with those communities that seek to implement such a scheme and where security permits, and de-mining has cleared significant agricultural areas and routes.

SUMMARY

UNOSOM I, UNITAF & UNOSOM II demonstrated the preparedness of the international community to aid a war-devastated land and how much could be achieved through co-ordinated international action. However the need for the majority of the indigenous people to support these external efforts is clear. Without such support the external UN forces cannot achieve a peaceful environment within a cost in terms of lives that is acceptable.

It must be recorded that the progress towards national political reconciliation is slow and without the will of the Somali Political groups to pursue a course of peaceful reconciliation, UNOSOM II cannot achieve further significant progress.

Therefore although the Force is mandated to remain until March 1995, the situation is constantly under review. The Force's size will probably be reduced gradually unless there is clearly no evidence of real progress on the Somali political scene in which case an earlier withdrawal might take place.

The operations of UNITAF and UNOSOM II demonstrate the difficulties of 'enforcing' peace from outside in the complex situation of a country with no clear single authority or existing structure but where a major power holder enjoying considerable local support refuses to co-operate. It may be that the difficulties of such 'enforcement action' were not fully appreciated by the external powers.

UNOSOM I, UNITAF & UNOSOM II : FACTS

Location: Somalia

Duration: April 1992 - to date; Currently mandated until March 1995 unless situation deteriorates in which case earlier withdrawal may take place.

Function: Create secure environment for humanitarian aid including disarming and control of weapons of warring parties.

Authorization: Recorded in the following UN Security Council Resolutions:

UNOSOM I

Resolution No Date	**Resolution**
751 (1992) 24/4/92	Establishes UN Operation in Somalia (UNOSOM) and a Committee to monitor arms embargo.
775 (1992) 28/8/92	Authorises further increase in UNOSOM strength as recommended by SG.

UNITAF

794 (1992) 3/12/92	Endorses SG's recommendation to take action under Chapter VII to ensure delivery of aid in Somalia.
814 (1993) 26/3/93	Requests SG to ensure delivery of aid to Somalia; strengthens and extends UNOSOM to 31 October 1993 to take over from UNITAF. In effect creates UNOSOM II.

UNOSOM II

814 (1993) 26/3/93	Requests SG to ensure delivery of aid to Somalia; strengthens and extends UNOSOM to 31 October 1993. In effect creates UNOSOM II.
837 (1993) 6/6/93	Condemns armed attacks against UNOSOM II personnel; SG authorised to take measure against those responsible.

865 (1993) 22/9/93	Condemns attacks on UNOSOM II personnel.
878 (1993) 29/10/93	Extends UNOSOM II to 18 Nov 1993.
885 (1993) 16/11/93	Establishes Commission of Enquiry to investigate armed attacks on UNOSOM II personnel.
886 (1993) 18/11/93	Extends UNOSOM II until 1 May 1994.
887 (1994)	Revised UNOSOM II mandate to exclude disarmament of factions or active intervention to stop inter-factional fighting. Mandate to end by March 1995.

Strength: UNOSOM I: Maximum- 550 Pakistani troops plus UNMOS & small HQW staff

UNITAF: Maximum - 37,000 (includes 8,000 US at sea). Force deployed as at 7/1/93:

USA	21,000
Belgium	572
Botswana	303
Canada	1,262
Egypt	270
France	2,783
Germany	60
Italy	2,150
Kuwait	43
Morocco	1,356
New Zealand	42
Saudi Arabia	643
Turkey	309
UK	90(??)

Plus Advance Parties from: Australia, India, Nigeria, Pakistan   Sweden, Tunisia, Zimbabwe.

UNOSOM II (as at November 1993)

Country	Description	Strength
Australia	Movement control	48
Bangladesh	Infantry battalion	945
Belgium	BDE HQ Infantry battalion	948
Botswana	Infantry company	326
Canada	Staff personnel	4
Egypt	Infantry battalions	1100
France	BDE HQ Infantry battalion Aviation unit Logistical battalion ————	
	Total, France	1107
Germany	Logistical units	1726
Greece	Medical unit	102
India	BDE HQ 3 Infantry battalions Total, India	4937
Ireland	Transport company	79
Italy	BDE HQ 3 Infantry battalions Aviation unit Logistical/engineering unit Medical unit ————	
	Total, Italy	2576
Kuwait	Infantry company	156
Malaysia	Infantry battalion	871
Morocco	Infantry battalion Support unit ———— Total	1424

Nepal	Security company	311
New Zealand	Supply unit	43
Nigeria	Recce battalion	614
Norway	Headquarters company	130 (140)
Pakistan	BDE HQ Infantry battalions 4 tank squadron Signal unit and Support —————— Total, Pakistan	5005
Republic of Korea 	Engineer battalion	252
Romania	Field hospital	236
Saudi Arabia	Infantry battalion	757
Sweden	Field hospital	148
Tunisia	Infantry company	142
Turkey	Infantry battalion	320
United Arab Emirates	Infantry battalion	662
United States	Logistical unit	3017
Zimbabwe	Infantry battalion Signal company	895 63
Military Police Company (composite)		100
Headquarters staff		240
	——————	
Grand Total		**29284**

(There were approximately 17,700 troops in the United States Joint Task Force in Somalia, which did not form part of UNOSOM II and were not under the operational command of the Force Commander of UNOSOM II. This number included the Quick Reaction Force (1,350), which was deployed in support of UNOSOM II.

UNOSOM II (as at July 1994)

Australia	Movement Control	66
Bangladesh	Inf Bn	975
Botswana	Inf Bn	425
Egypt	Inf Bn x 3	1683
India	Inf Bde x 4 bn	4975
Indonesia	HQ Support	4
Ireland	Logistic Support	93
South Korea	HQ Support Unit	6
Malaysia	Inf Bn+	1089
Nepal	Security Company	314
New Zealand	Supply Unit	50
Nigeria	Security Bn	745
Pakistan	Bde: 4 x inf bn Tank Regt heli sqn	7152
Romania	Field Hospital	231
Zimbabwe	Inf Bn + Sig coy	1095
Total		**18903**

Costs:

Cost authorised by UN $84,700,000 gross per month for the period 1 November 1993- 28 February 1994.

Estimated 1/11/93-31/3/94 $413.5 million, and expenses so far for UNOSOM I and UNOSOM II total $765 million.

The estimated cost for UNOSOM II for 6 months was $856,355.000.

UNAMIC
&
UNTAC

POLITICAL BACKGROUND

In late 1953 Cambodia achieved independence, having previously been a part of French Indo-China. Over the next 17 years the country was governed by the administration headed by Prince Sihanouk which had to contend with opposition from forces of both right and left wing parties operating in the country. However in March 1970 Sihanouk was ousted by General Nol and Sihanouk then, in cooperation with the Khmer Rouge, established a government in exile.

After five years of armed insurrection led by the Khmer Rouge, in which an estimated 700,000 people died and some 2 million were made homeless, the Khmer Rouge overthrew Nol and formed their own administration under the Prime Minister 'Pol Pot'. This did not end the country's troubles as when the Khmer Rouge extended their ruthless regime into an ethnically Khmer part of Vietnam, Vietnamese forces invaded Cambodia in December 1978 and installed a regime favourable to them, while the Khmer Rouge withdrew to isolated areas to wage a guerrilla war against the government installed by the Vietnamese. In addition to the Khmer Rouge's military force called the National Army of Democratic Kampuchea (NADK), the new government, the PRK and its Cambodian People's Armed Forces (CPAF), faced guerrilla attacks from two other smaller factions - the National Army of Independent Kampuchea (ANKI) and the People's National Liberation Armed Forces (KPNLAF).

UN INVOLVEMENT

In July 1989 after lengthy negotiations an international conference on Cambodia opened in Paris. With the close involvement of the permanent members of the UN Security Council and a number of 'false dawns', after protracted negotiations a Comprehensive Political Settlement was signed between the parties on 23 October 1991. A major feature of the Agreement was the inclusion of an annexe dealing with the role for a UN peace-keeping force in Cambodia which it was hoped would in effect oversee the country's administration during the period prior to free elections and the creation of a new democratic government.

In late August-early September 1991 a UN Survey Mission of six civilian and six military UN Secretarial staff visited Cambodia, and in September 1991, aware of this proposed task for the UN, the SecretaryGeneral recommended that a small UN 'Advanced Mission' should be sent to Cambodia to evaluate how a UN force could best fulfil the requests of the parties meeting in Paris for UN help with the implementation of the Peace Agreement. The creation of the United Nations Advance Mission to Cambodia (UNAMIC) was agreed by Resolution 717 (1991) on 16 October 1991.

UNAMIC

UNAMIC was to be formally established immediately after the signing of the Peace Agreement and was intended to provide a number of military and civilian UN personnel to help monitor and maintain the cease-fire, primarily by acting as liaison officers with the military headquarters of the four parties and from its own Headquarters at the capital Phnom Penh. In addition the Mission was to consider the creation of a mine-awareness programme to help cope with the major problem of the estimated 600,000 mines scattered across the country. UNAMIC would also cooperate closely with the staff from the UN High Commission for Refugees (UNHCR). The Mission was to consist of some 200 persons both civil and military, among the latter being 50 Military Observers (UNMOs) with a further 40 military communications staff and a mine-awareness team 20 strong.

UNAMIC, although created under UN Security Council Resolution 717 of 16 October 1991, was not actually mentioned as such in the Paris Peace Agreements and as a result the Khmer Rouge and its armed elements refused in many instances to recognize UNAMIC as a legitimate agency of the UN. This was a major obstacle as clearly the work of UNAMIC would require the cooperation of all the Cambodian parties, particularly with regard to freedom of movement around the country.

Following the formal signing of the Peace Agreement in Paris on 23 October, the UN, on 31 October, welcomed the Agreement and requested the SecretaryGeneral to continue to prepare for the subsequent establishment of a UN Transitional Authority in Cambodia (UNTAC) which would build on UNAMIC's earlier work.

UNAMIC became operational on 9 November 1991 with personnel drawn from 22 member states. In January 1992 under Resolution 728 (1992) UNAMIC's Mandate was extended to include the training of Cambodian mine-clearing teams and to initiate a mine-clearance, rather than merely a mine-awareness, programme. As a result of this extension of the Mandate a further three member states provided additional personnel for UNAMIC.

Apart from the Military Observers and Liaison Officers, there were small national contingents providing the logistic support infrastructure: air transportation (French); Communications (Australian); Medical support (German); Mine-Awareness (New Zealand. Once the mine-awareness programme expanded to include mine-clearing, a Thai engineer battalion joined UNAMIC to carry out major route clearance, with a second Thai battalion also in-country under a bilateral Thai-Cambodian agreement. The final total military strength of UNAMIC was some 884 with 144 civilian staff.

Within UNAMIC there were problems of operational and administrative inter-face between the UN civilian and military personnel, primarily owing to the lack of clear standard procedures and working practices: much was made in the media of the civilian 'nine-to-five' five day week as opposed to the military seven days a week schedule. A further problem was the need for a common language within the Mission with a number of UNMOs speaking no English - the most commonly used language - and almost inevitably few members spoke or could understand the language of Cambodia.

UNTAC

With UNAMIC in situ, the UN SecretaryGeneral reported to the Security Council on the provision of UNTAC early in 1992 and under Resolution 745 (1992) of 28 February 1992 the Security Council established UNTAC for a period not exceeding 18 months. On its establishment UNTAC was to absorb UNAMIC.

UNTAC had seven main functional tasks. The most manpower intensive of these were those allotted to the peace-keeping component under the military force commander (Lt General J Sanderson). This component was tasked with the verification of the withdrawal from and nonreturn to Cambodia of all foreign troops; supervision of the ceasefire, including investigation of alleged breaches or noncompliance by a party; the 'cantonment', ie disarming, and the demobilisation of the majority of the military forces of the Cambodian parties. This work included the storage of arms thus surrendered and other weapons found during searches of areas, as well as monitoring the cessation of external arms shipments. These tasks were seen as crucial to the Peace Process so that the registration of voters could take place in a secure environment. Further the military force was responsible for the mine-clearance training programmes.

The UN police component (UNCIVPOL) was to help reestablish and supervise the local police force to ensure law and order was impartially maintained and, in addition for ensuring that the human rights requirements were also achieved. The UN police, although separate from the military, worked closely with them. Further components of UNTAC were assisting with the civilian administration of the country; preparing the country for free, UN supervised, elections; as well as working on rehabilitation and repatriation measures in conjunction with the UNHCR and nongovernment agencies (NGOs). With some 350,000 refugees and displaced persons in camps along the Thai-Cambodian border, this was a major task of particular importance if the elections were to be genuinely representative.

The planning for the actual deployment of UNTAC began in November 1991 when a small mission visited Cambodia and UNAMIC. This work established that there were some 203,000 regular troops from the four parties that would need cantonment and subsequent action, all but 70% were to be demobilised after the election. The size of UN force required was considered to be 15,900: 12 infantry battalions, military observers, and logistics support particularly engineers, medical troops, communications and naval and air elements: the latter consisting respectively of 32 vessels from the Cambodian navy, 10 fixed-wing aircraft and 26 helicopters.

With the arrival of the SecretaryGeneral's Special Representative and the Force Commander in Phnom Penh on 15 March 1992, UNTAC came formally into being. The Force Commander now reevaluated the proposed force deployment and cantonment plan in the light of the circumstances then prevailing on the ground and the plan was finalised at the end of May 1992. The country was divided into a number of sectors, some with sub-sectors and with Phnom Penh as a 'Special Zone' where the Force Headquarters was based. The number of cantonment sites was finally fixed at some 86 with 62 for the CPAF, 15 for NADK, five for the ANKI and four for the KPNLAF (Map 1).

The second phase of the implementation of the Peace Agreement - the cantonment process - was due to begin on 13 June 1992 when it was expected that eight battalions would have been deployed. However the slow build up of UNTAC troops, hindered by the limited communications infrastructure within Cambodia, meant that by that date, although all UNTAC units were incountry at various strengths, only four battalions were fully-deployed to their sectors with all equipment and able to start the cantonment.

The Khmer Rouge, claiming that Vietnamese forces were still in the country, and that the pro-Vietnamese administration was still in control in Phnom Penh, refused to co-operate with UNTAC in the cantonment of its NADK troops or to grant UNTAC full access to the areas under NADK control. Nevertheless in spite of this, by mid-July, all UNTAC infantry were deployed albeit not fully in NADK areas, and some 18,500 troops had been cantoned. Over the next few months the totals steadily increased so that by 21 September more than 50,000 troops from the other three parties had been cantoned and 38,000 of those from the CPAF had accepted 'agricultural leave' to help harvest the rice crop. In excess of 50,000 weapons were under UN control. UN troops were also conducting regular patrols to detect and discourage unauthorised troop movements, searching for arms caches and deterring 'banditry'

Using some 700 UNMOs, checkpoints had been established on the borders with Vietnam, Laos and Thailand as well as at the airports, on the main incountry routes including naval teams on key waterways, and at the port of Sihanoukville. These absorbed checkpoints established earlier by UNAMIC. The Observation teams consisted of 4/5 men plus an interpreter and in certain areas plus a UNCIVPOL presence. In addition there were three 'foreign liaison teams' in the capitals of Thailand, Laos and Vietnam. .

However the difficulties with the Khmer Rouge and the NADK created additional problems with its main opponent the PRK which considered that the NADK was taking the opportunity of the Cantonment process to extend its area of influence. The PRK blamed UNTAC for not coercing NADK and responding forcefully by arresting the Khmer Rouge leader for genocide. As a result of the high tension between these two parties there were a considerable number of cease-fire violations with both NADK and CPAF being involved in fire-fights including mortar and artillery exchanges. These violations further hindered the completion of the cantonment exercise as arms had to be released on some occasions to cantoned troops under the right to self-defence permitted to all parties by the Peace Agreement. In addition there had been some instances of fire being directed at UNTAC helicopters, apparently from NADK areas. The obstruction by the Khmer Rouge and the NADK was condemned by Resolution 766 (1992) of 21 July 1992 which also directed that the benefits of UN rehabilitation aid should only go to those parties co-operating with UNTAC.

In spite of this problem and the instability it created in some areas, on the repatriation front six refugee centres were set up and considerable progress was made so that by late September 1992 some 115,000 refugees had returned and by May 1993 370,000. The manning of these centres as well as the provision of escorts for UNHCR convoys both from neighbouring countries to the reception centres and subsequently for convoys of processed refugees on to their final destination, fell to the military force for most of the period.

The mineclearing work was also in hand. The first course began on 24 February 1992 under UNAMIC and by May 1993 a total of 183 personnel drawn from eight nations had trained more than 2,000 Cambodians, about 600 of whom were currently employed on mineclearing. In the period up to May 1993 some 15,000 mines had been cleared.

The Paris Agreements envisaged that the cantonment and demobilisation process would be completed by September 1992 with the registration of voters ready to begin in November. By October it was apparent that as the cantonment had not succeeded, full demobilisation too was impossible. However it was essential to begin the electoral registration process if the elections were to be held as scheduled in May 1993 and Resolution 792 (1992) of 30 November 1992 reaffirmed that the elections would go ahead at that date and called for the denial of petroleum products to parties not complying with the military provisions of the Paris Agreement. However the vastness of the area dominated by the NADK made the complete enforcement of this resolution impractical, although the UNTAC checkpoints and ground and air patrols did apparently have some effect.

The UNTAC civilian electoral teams were physically escorted by UNTAC military in more dangerous areas while relying on general UNTAC patrols in safer areas. Initially the electoral sectors' boundaries did not conform exactly with those of the military sectors with resultant problems of coordination and control, so in December 1992 the military boundaries were readjusted to overcome this problem. In spite of the lack of full cooperation by the NADK, there was no serious or consistent disruption of the registration process, although there were instances when UNTAC personnel were temporarily detained or threatened by NADK forces. Nevertheless 95% of eligible voters were registered. Further, with UN civil advisers present in the administrative structure of the three other Cambodian parties who were cooperating, human rights and civilian police matters were under way in almost all of the country's 21 civilian provinces.

In the run-up to the elections violence in some areas became more intense. After the beginning of the dry season in November 1992 there were some serious clashes between the NADK and the CPAF, one in instance of shelling 15,000 civilians fled from their homes. However the first clearly deliberate attack on UNTAC took place on 27 March 1993 when one Bangladeshi soldier was killed. Then from late April there were four more deliberate attacks in which a further UNTAC soldier was killed and nine others wounded. The NADK was implicated in these attacks. As a result UNTAC took steps to provide its posts with better defences and enhanced protection.

In spite of the difficulties, particularly the refusal of the Khmer Rouge party to cooperate with UNTAC in either the demobilisation of its force the NADK, or to permit UNTAC troops and electoral teams free access to areas under its control, UNTAC's presence helped give the voters confidence that these were genuinely democratic elections and attempts at disruption of the elections failed to have any significant effect. The 89% turnout of voters reflected this achievement. The elections between 23 and 28 May were certified as free and fair by the international observers.

The result was that no party won a clear majority but the two main contenders, the Royalist party (FUNCINPEC) with 45% of the vote and the previously ruling KPP with 38% were clearly the most powerful. Initial objections from the KPP and claims of malpractice were defused by UNTAC's agreement to investigate these and the leader of the KPP stated publicly that he had no intention of rejecting the election. The elected Constituent Assembly met first on 14 June 1993 and at the request of the Cambodian parties, UNTAC provided logistical and operational assistance as well as technical advice to the Assembly. The results of the election were endorsed by the Security Council in Resolution 84 (1993) of 15 June 1993. After the two main parties, with 109 seats in the 120 seat Constituent Assembly, agreed to co-operate in forming a new interim administration, in late June the Khmer Rouge indicated that they might be prepared to co-operate with the interim administration. However pre-conditions for such co-operation were not agreed by the new government and a low-level guerrilla campaign by the Khmer Rouge has continued. Nevertheless, the new administration has control of the majority of the country.

WITHDRAWAL

The withdrawal plan for the UNTAC military force was in three phases with the first consisting of preparations in situ by units scheduled to withdraw. With the second phase, which took place in early August 1993 there was an initial thinning out of the military contingents by battalion. As each infantry battalion withdrew, along with its associated medical, engineering and other units, so the battalion in the neighbouring sector redeployed to cover the vacated area. The third phase from 1 September-15 November with four subordinate stages would cover the successive withdrawals of the remaining infantry and other units.

The Headquarters, Communications and UN Observers, both military and naval were to withdraw as their tasks were completed, the observers drawing inwards to the centres of the appropriate provinces and then reducing in numbers.

The UNCIVPOL force similarly reduced in strength from July with the last of the 3,600 leaving in mid-October 1993. The other civilian components reduced as their services were no longer needed, apart from the few designated to remain with the UN civilian office.

With Resolution 860 (1993) of 27 August 1993 the Security Council endorsed the SecretaryGeneral's plan for the withdrawal of UNTAC and confirmed that UNTAC's functions should end on the creation of a new government of Cambodia. This duly took place on 24 of September with the promulgation of a constitution for Cambodia as a constitutional monarchy with a legislative assembly. This confirmed the successful implementation of the mandate of UNTAC.

Nevertheless, in spite of UNTAC's success, there was still a considerable level of 'banditry' in outlying areas. Therefore the Commander of the remaining UNTAC forces recommended that military personnel were still required to protect UN civilian staff trying to recover UN equipment. Accordingly under Resolution 860 (1993) the retention was authorised until the end of 1993 of a small force of military police with some medical support.

A further force of some 20 Liaison Officers was also requested by the Royal Cambodian government to assist in the residual military matters and help maintain public confidence in security matters. This body was authorised under Resolution 880(1993), the personnel being drawn largely from ex-UNTAC members with 15 separate countries contributing personnel. The Secretary-General was firm that as the UN Peace-keeping operation had been concluded, it would be better to keep a 'one-off' unit such as these LOs separate from the civilian UN office that was to remain in Cambodia to assist in peace-building measures.

SUMMARY

Despite the difficulties faced by UNTAC, the mandate can be said to have been successfully achieved. Fair and free elections were held in Cambodia in spite of opposition from a major party which, although still not co-operating with the new democratic administration, has not seriously disrupted the move towards a stable society.

UNAMIC/UNTAC : FACTS

Location: Cambodia

Duration: Initially for not more than 18 months (effectively for about
                       6 months after election).

Function: Oversee cease-fire, disarm & demobilize; monitor human rights;
                       oversee national administration until free elections; assist
                       election process and monitor elections; humanitarian.

Authorization: Recorded in the following UN Security Council Resolutions:

Resolution No Date	**Resolution**
717 (1991) 16/10/91	Noting Peace Agreement, decides to establish UN Advanced Mission in Cambodia calls on all parties to co-operate with this Mission (UNAMIC)
728 (1992) 8/1/92	Extends UNAMIC's Mandate to include training for mine-clearing & initiation of mine-clearing programme.
745(1992) 28/2/92	Establishes UNTAC for not more than 18 months; states that it is vital that elections be held by May 1993.
766(1992) 21/7/92	Expresses deep concern at refusal of one party to co-operate with UNTAC
783(1992) 13/10/92	Deplores the non-compliance by the PDK with its obligations. Confirms that elections will be held by May 1993.
792(1992) 30/11/92	Condemns PDK for failure to comply with its obligations. Calls for ban on oil supplies to all parties not complying with the Peace Agreement requirements.
810(1993) 8/3/1993	Endorses decision for elections in May. Urges all parties to take all measures to ensure free and fair elections.
826 (1993) 20/5/93	Expresses satisfaction with arrangements for election of Constituent Assembly in Cambodia.

835 (1993)	Considers that elections in Cambodia 3/6/93 were free and calls on parties to respect results.
840 (1993) 15/6/93	Endorses results of Cambodian elections; requests UNTAC to continue role during transition.
860 (1993) 27/8/93	Establishes timetable for ending of mandate and withdrawal of UNTAC from Cambodia.
880 (1993) 4/11/93	Approves timetable of UNTAC withdrawal from Cambodia.

Strength: (Maximum) Military - formed units & HQ: 15,191 UNMOs 476

Contributors: In all 46 countries contributed troops or police personnel.
Military contributions from:
Australia, Austria, Bangladesh (bn),
Bulgaria (bn), Canada, China (engr bn),
Chile, France(bn+log), Germany (med),
Ghana(2xbn), India (2xbn), Indonesia(2xbn),
Ireland, Japan(engr bn), Malaysia(bn)
Namibia, the Netherlands(bn), New Zealand,
Pakistan(bn), the Philippines, Poland,
the Russian Federation, Singapore,
Thailand(engr bn), Tunisia(bn), Uruguay(bn),
the United Kingdom, United States of America.

Costs: UNAMIC/UNTAC 1.11.91-30.9.93: US$1,523,696,000

Proportions:

Military	32.7%;
Civilian	26.6%
Air Operations	8.2%
Transport	7.2%
Premises	8.6%
Communications	4.0%
Naval	0.4%
Freight	3.1%
Other Supplies	5.5%
Other Programmes	2.4%
Infrastructure	0.4%
Others	0.9%

Casualties: Died   Wounded

	Died	Wounded
Civilian	3	1
Civpol	3	7
Local civ	23	6
Military	39	43
UNMOs	3	1
UN Vols	2	0

Military Personnel Costs in Thousands:

    a.   Military Observers: 64,162.9

    b.   Military Contingent   376,759.5

    Others costed for b.   57,220.0

Civilian Personnel:

    a.   Civpol   204,764.6

    b.   International & Local Staff   183,705.0

    c.   UN Volunteers   16,199.0

UNPROFOR

UNITED NATIONS PROTECTION FORCE (UNPROFOR)

INTRODUCTION

United Nations' troops are deployed in three separate yet related operations in the territory of the former Federal Republic of Yugoslavia. Working alongside the UN is a smaller mission established by the EEC, while other regional security bodies such as NATO and CSCE are also co-operating with the UN's mission.

ORIGIN OF CONFLICT

Following the death in 1980 of Tito the long-standing President of Yugoslavia, there was a period of gradual change from the doctrine of one-party rule which had secured some measure of ethnic harmony among the various constituent Republics and ethnic groups that made up Yugoslavia: the republics of Serbia, Bosnia-Herzegovina, Croatia, Slovenia, Macedonia and Montenegro. The period of change became more rapid and volatile in the mid-1980s when a more populist and clearly nationalist theme began to dominate Serbian party attitudes. This caused concern among the other national groupings within the other Republics of Yugoslavia, particularly as to many, the Serbs were closely identified with the controlling Communist Federal regime.

Discussions between the constituent republics on the future structure and on bids for self-government by various ethnic minorities, eg Serbs in Croatia, failed to reach any practical and universally accepted solutions. Free multi-party elections brought nation-alist governments to power in Slovenia, Croatia and Bosnia-Herzogovina.
Attempts by the Federal authorities to dissuade secession by republics by use of the Yugoslav Peoples' Army (Federal Army, JNA), led in June 1991 to fighting in Slovenia. Further, ethnic groups of Serbs in Croatia sought to establish independence and in effect to join Serbia; this led to fierce fighting in Croatia from July 1991.

PEACE EFFORTS : SLOVENIA

Initial efforts to end the fighting were undertaken under the aegis of the EEC with agreement from the CSCE forum which delegated the task to the EEC. The Slovenian situation was stabilised by the European Community's plan of July 8 1991 whereby the Federal Army withdrew to barracks, while Slovenia and Croatia suspended further independence moves for three months. The EEC provided a limited number of monitors (ECMM), who arrived on 15 July, to oversee the accord. This agreement held in Slovenia where the Serbs in particular had no ethnic minority interest in stopping the republic's secession. However in withdrawing, the Serb-officered Federal Army did hand over considerable quantities of heavy weapons to Serb irregular forces in Croatia.

PEACE EFFORTS : CROATIA

However in Croatia the cease-fire was rarely observed as the Croats sought to reassert control of Serb dominated areas and 150 EEC Monitors who arrived in early September were powerless to halt the conflict. As a result, on 25 September the UN imposed an arms embargo on all factions and as the threat of fresh fighting in Croatia increased, the EEC agreed to double the size of its monitor force.

The EEC-sponsored peace conference which had re-convened at the Hague on 7 September, put forward a plan with the aim of providing 'sovereign and independent Republics for those which wish it' as well as 'special status for certain groups and areas'. This last however was seen as unacceptable to Serbia, fearing for its Serb enclaves in Croatia and there were further Federal Army attacks in Croatia throughout October. The EC threatened Serbia with sanctions if its attacks continued and the UN Security Council imposed sanctions and an arms embargo on the whole of former Yugoslavia by Resolution 713 (1991) of 25 September 1991.

On November 4 Serbia rejected the EC's ultimatum, but on 19 of that month at French brokered talks, both sides agreed to the demilitarization of Dubrovnik then under heavy Serbian attack and on 23 November, another cease-fire (the 14th) was agreed. However the emphasis switched now to the UN Security Council and on 25 and 28 November 1991 Croatia and Serbia respectively agreed to the deployment of UN peacekeepers should these be forthcoming.

In response, on 15 December the UN Security Council voted to send a peace-keeping force but as the first UN Military Observer/Monitors (UNMOs) arrived in Zagreb on 26 of the same month, fighting was again underway in Croatia. The Croats appeared to see the intervention of the UN as a means of regaining its lost territories, while the Serbs saw it as a means of keeping the Serbian enclaves in Croatia out of Croat hands.

On 21 February 1992 the UN Security Council passed Resolution 743 establishing a United Nations Protective Force (UNPROFOR) with a 12 month mandate to create the conditions of peace and security required for the negotiation of an overall settlement to the Yugoslav crisis in accordance with a UN-sponsored peace-keeping plan, the focus being at that time still Croatia.

The peace-keeping plan rested on two central elements:

a.   withdrawal of the Federal Army (JNA) from all of Croatia and the demilitari-sation of the three 'UN Protected Areas' (UNPAs) in Croatia, corresponding largely to areas where inter-communal tensions had led to armed conflict.

b.   continuing function on an interim basis of existing local authorities under UN supervision pending the achievement of an overall political settlement under the auspices of the EEC's Conference on Yugoslavia.

Further aims of the peace-plan and UNPROFOR's deployment were the re-establish-ment of local police forces and associated matters to create the necessary normalization of life. This would be carried out in co-operation with the UN High Commissioner for Refugees (UNHCR) overseeing the return of refugees displaced by the fighting. UNPROFOR was deployed to the UNPAs with an additional number of UN Civil Police (UNCIVPOL) to monitor local police actions. UNPROFOR was to remain impartial and 'normally' only use minimum force in self-defence. (The EEC Monitoring Teams remained in situ and were to work in close co-operation with UNPROFOR). The duration of UNPROFOR's mandate was 12 months - double the usual period for a UN Peace-Keeping Force.

The UN Security Council on 15 May 1992 set out the measures by which the grounds for a political settlement could be achieved, these rested largely on the cessation of violent means to achieve political change and the effective restoration of the status quo before the recent fighting. When the Resolution was ignored by Serbia and Montenegro, economic sanctions were imposed by Resolution 757 (1992) of 30 May 1992.

Subsequently on 30 June under Resolution 779 (1992) the UN Force was authorised to assist in the formation of a Joint Commission to oversee the progressive return of the "pink zones" (areas of Serb control outside the UNPAs) to Croatian control. This required the demilitarization of local irregulars and the storage of heavy weapons in UN monitored locations. UNCIVPOL were to monitor the activities of the Croatian and local police forces in their law and order tasks, and the latter's structure to be compatible with local demographic structure prior to the conflict. Further on 7 August, UNPROFOR's mandate was extended to cover the establishment of border controls at international crossing points leading into the UNPAs to monitor movement of embargoed items.

The Force's Mandate was further extended by Resolution 779 (1992) of 6 October 1992 to oversee the demilitarization of a key area: the Prevlaka Peninsula area and the withdrawal of the Yugoslav Peoples' Army, and to take control of the Peruca Dam - actually taken under UNPROFOR control on 14 September.

At the same time the UN and the EC jointly convened a conference in London which brought together all the main parties of the former Yugoslavia and a broad range of ministers from the international community. Apart from establishing certain commitments on principles as a basis for a final settlement, it established the UN/EC co-chairmanship of the International Conference on Former Yugoslavia (ICFY) to carry the detailed work forward.

UNPROFOR IN CROATIA

UNPROFOR's force drawn from 26 countries, deployed into Croatia covering four sectors (Map 1), its strength rose by February 1993 to just under 14,000 men. With regard to the implementation of the various elements of UNPROFOR's mandate, almost from the outset, the Serbs in Croatia refused to accept UNPROFOR controls at the international borders and they opposed the concept of Croatia regulating the commerce of the UNPAs: this they considered would be a breach of the peace-keeping plan. Within the UNPAs themselves the situation worsened even after the deployment of UNPROFOR. Persecution of minority groups, murders and other assaults led UNPROFOR to establish 'protected villages' in the autumn and winter of 1992 and, in the last resort, to re-locate several hundred vulnerable civilians to Croatia. This situation was totally at variance with the perceived role for UNPROFOR in reintegrating Croat & Serb communities.

In January 1993 the Croats made a heavy attack on parts of the UNPAs and 'Pink Zones' resulting in a fresh escalation of fighting, with the Serbs then recovering heavy weapons they had stored under UN supervision. The UN and the International Conference sought to broker effective cease-fires and a permanent political solution in Croatia. However the two sides refused to compromise. UNPROFOR was blamed by both sides for its failure to fulfil their expectations: on the Croat side the restoration of 'normal' conditions (ie restoration of Croat overall control) and the return of refugees; on the Serb side, the protection of Serb minority areas against Croat aggression and control. As an example of this attitude, in early April the Serbs told the Deputy Chief of Mission that although they would have liked to accept UNPROFOR as a genuine protection force, its behaviour led them to tend to see it as a 'partial' body and therefore a 'hostile presence'.

As a result both Serbs and Croats placed restrictions on the movement of UNPROFOR. UNMOs and UNCIVPOL were unable to move freely outside main towns and the normal passage of both humanitarian and logistical convoys was obstructed by the closing of crossing-points. In addition restrictions were placed on UNPROFOR aerial movements with even reconnaissance flights only being possible after detailed negotiations for air corridors.

In addition the various elements of the warring sides frequently acted independently of their supposed command chain with the effect that UNPROFOR could never be certain that pre-negotiated agreements, or orders supporting UNPROFOR activities would be honoured by any group with whom they came into contact.

From the spring of 1993 there was a sharp escalation in the level of hostile acts against UNPROFOR resulting in the death of several members of the Force (by September 1993 UNPROFOR had suffered 357 casualties in Croatia of which 31 were killed).

By the autumn of 1993, although UNPROFOR remained in place, its mandate having been renewed, there had been little progress towards any 'normalization' of life in the "pink zones" or the UNPAs, certainly as far as the return of Displaced Persons and re-creation of pre-conflict administrative structures. The local authorities both Serb and Croat had resisted the efforts of UNPROFOR to forward these aims. Both sides made representations to the UN complaining of the other's actions in breach of UN Resolutions.

At the end of 1993, the UN Secretary-General reported that the efforts of the International Conference had developed a more positive attitude and indeed in many of the UNPAs, steps to normalise social and economic life had been taken as well as positive attempts to achieve a cessation of hostilities. This latter aspect was heavily reliant on local initiatives ranging from formal signed cease-fire agreements in the Eastern UNPROFOR Sector, to oral, unsigned but implemented 'gentleman's agreements' in the other three Sectors.

Local cease-fires were supplemented by additional UNMOs' patrols and the installation of 'hot-lines' between the opposing commanders. These steps achieved a subsequent reduction in tension and violations. However such steps were easily undermined, for example in late October the Croats deployed 'Special Police' elements into one of the UNPROFOR sectors which heightened tensions and caused the suspension of inter-factional negotiations: these police were withdrawn three weeks later after strenuous efforts by UNPROFOR.

The improvements in the area permitted UNPROFOR to concentrate more on identifying the most essential humanitarian aid targets in the region. This was carried out in conjunction with the other agencies involved, the UNHCR, ECMM, and ICRC, through a Joint Humanitarian Cell. But again progress towards economic and social gains between the two sides varied from area to area: in some, local agreements could be reached regardless of the state of higher level affairs, while in others, the lack of higher level progress resulted in total refusal at lower levels to discuss any related matters.

In March 1994 a new cease-fire was agreed between the Croatian and Serbian sides and although there were local difficulties in some areas, by the end of May there had been general compliance. UNPROFOR controlled a 'separation zone' of some 1,300 sq km and most heavy weapons were now in agreed storage sites.

Although there was Croat dissatisfaction with the slow progress in resolving rehabilitation and control aspects of certain areas under Serbian control which had led to the former to threaten attacks, the situation was more stable.

SUMMARY

In the Croatian area of UNPROFOR operations, the importance of local liaison and confidence building measures was clearly demonstrated. Although there remains much to be achieved in returning the area to normality, UNPROFOR has helped to stabilise the situation and effect a general reduction in the level of violence.

BOSNIA & HERZOGOVINA

Until the end of 1991 the multi-ethnic republic of Bosnia-Herzogovina had avoided internal armed unrest. Nevertheless in October 1991 the EEC Monitoring mission's mandate was extended to cover Bosnia with the aim of helping to maintain peace and, if hostilities did occur, by investigating and reporting the facts, thus to help prevent rumour and distortion that might otherwise exacerbate the problem. The HQ of UNPROFOR was also established in Bosnia (at Sarajevo) as this provided a base unaffected by the Croatian conflict. It was hoped too that its presence would serve as a stabilizing factor.

The international recognition of Bosnia as an independent state in April 1992 led to a sharp polarisation of the ethnic groups within Bosnia and Herzegovina (the population being divided approximately along the following lines: Muslims 43%, Serbs 32%, Croats 25%), with subsequent isolated incidents escalating into full-scale war. As a result of the EC's recognition of Bosnia, the ECMM found itself deemed 'unfriendly' by Bosnian Serbs opposed to the planned independent Bosnian state and some Monitoring Teams had to be withdrawn.

Similarly UNPROFOR was forced to move its HQ from Bosnia in May but some 120 UNPROFOR personnel were left in Sarajevo. This group increasingly undertook negotiations on ad hoc problems between the warring parties and assisted as far as possible, with humanitarian efforts.

After UNPROFOR in early June 1992 had negotiated the re-opening of Sarajevo airport for humanitarian aid flights, by Resolution 761(92) of 29.6.92., UNPROFOR was mandated to take over full responsibility for the airport, as well as the monitoring of the centralisation of certain heavy weapons systems of the warring parties within Bosnia. A force level allocated for this task was some 1,900 troops including French, Ukranian and Egyptian units. Subsequently under Resolution 776(92) of 14.9.92. UNPROFOR was tasked to support the humanitarian aid efforts of UNHCR, including the provision of military protection to aid convoys and the movements of wounded/refugees etc. In order to fulfil this task a separate Bosnia-Herzogovina Command of UNPROFOR was now established with an initial force level of some 7,800 additional troops; among these were units from the UK, France, Spain and Canada.

Subsequently a ban on military flights in Bosnia was established by Resolution 781(92) of 9.10.92. UNPROFOR was tasked to place observers as necessary at airfields - some 75 additional UNMOs being authorized for this task, with which the ECMM teams also co-operated. NATO also allocated AWACS and interceptors to assist with this monitoring under the code-name 'Operation DENY FLIGHT'. This action and the subsequent activities of the monitoring teams and the NATO air forces effectively ended fixed-wing combat sorties in the area by the warring factions and a reduction in other combat air activity by helicopter forces.

However there were continued helicopter movements and as at 22 September 1994 there had been some 2,200 recorded violations of the 'no flying' ban, mainly by helicopters being used for resupply or troop movement tasks sometimes being linked improperly by the participants with authorised medical tasks. In such instances flights on approved medical evacuation missions fail to stick to the agreed route and UN Military Observers have been refused access to inspect the aircraft. Although the identity of the violator has often been established, poor weather has on occasion prevented the necessary visual identification of the violator and the UN Secretary-General in reporting to the Security Council in March 1994, noted that these helicopter movements - "flying trucks" - were of little military significance and that the nature and specific circumstances of such flights had not so far justified shooting any of them down. It was clear that all parties to the conflict are guilty of flight violations. However on 28 February 1994 aircraft constituting what was only the second identified violation by combat aircraft since 'Op DENY FLIGHT' started, were intercepted by NATO aircraft and the violating aircraft were shot down.

At the end of 1992 the Co-Chairmen of the ICFY, Lord Owen and Cyrus Vance, drew up a peace plan for Bosnia based on the general principles agreed in late August 1992 by all the participants at the Conference in London. The UN Secretary-General noted that the package provided the only mechanism available for the re-establishment of peace in Bosnia and Herzogovina, with justice and respect for human rights. Under the interim agreements which covered all aspects of the restoration of normal political activity and civilian life, the specific military agreement detailed arrangements for the cessation of hostilities, separation of forces, demilitarization of Sarajevo and the opening of communication routes with repair to the infra-structure. This Agreement was signed by all three parties, the last, the Bosnian Government, signing on 3 March.

As a result, anticipating the need to provide the resources to implement and 'police' the ICFY Peace Plan, NATO set in hand contingency planning and it was suggested that some 64,000-75,000 troops might be required to <u>implement</u> the full plan: there was no consideration of seeking to <u>enforce</u> it.

However despite the Agreement, fighting continued in Bosnia, particularly in the Central Region with the result that humanitarian aid supplies to the area were considerably disrupted. In response the United States undertook an airdrop operation in late February and March 1993 to provide relief supplies to beleaguered areas such as Srebenica, Zepa, Konjevic and Gorazde. In due course this operation received additional supplies for dropping from a number of European nations.

Negotiations had continued between the three Bosnian parties on the Vance-Owen Peace Plan and with the signing of two outstanding papers by the Bosnian Serb leader on 2 May all three sides had agreed. However the Serb leader subsequently announced that the plan must be ratified by the Bosnian Serb self-styled 'Assembly' which refused ratification.

The situation in Central Bosnia continued to deteriorate as the fighting intensified between the Bosnian Serbs and the isolated pockets of other parties, despite efforts of UNPROFOR to push humanitarian aid through both by ground convoys and helicopter sorties, the latter however being aborted on a number of occasions by artillery fire directed against the landing zones.

In April 1993 under Resolution 819(93) the Security Council decided to send a mission to check the situation with Bosnia & Herzogovina which in due course recommended the creation of 'safe areas' for ethnic minorities. Subsequently under Resolution 824(93) of 6.5.93. certain towns: notably Srebenica, Zepa and Gorazde, Tuzla, Bihac as well as Sarajevo itself, all in the Bosnian Serb dominated region, were so designated with an UNPROFOR presence provided by 50 UN Military Observers to monitor their safety.

Subsequently under Resolution 836(1993) of 4 June 1993 UNPROFOR's mandate was extended to enable it to deter attacks against Safe Areas and to occupy some key points on the ground in efforts to monitor the conflict and promote the withdrawal of the rival military and para-military factions. As a result of this increased commitment Resolution 844 (1993) of 18 June authorised the reinforcement of UNPROFOR to permit the deployment to the Safe Areas of some 6,500 troops consisting of 4 mechanized infantry battalions for the Safe Areas and 1 for route control supported by an armoured reconnaissance battalion and commensurate logistic support units. The infantry presence in Sarajevo was also to be increased by a further 1,100 men.

However there was naturally a time-lag between the decision to deploy these additional forces and their arrival on the ground. In the interim the fighting in Central Bosnia continued with a more offensive posture from the Bosnian Government forces as the autumn wore on. In spite of a call from the UN Security Council on 9 November 1993 for all parties to assist the humanitarian aid distribution and to avoid actions exacerbating the situation, the fighting continued and this had a detrimental effect on the delivery of humanitarian supplies by road. Of particular concern to the UN were incidents such as that of early November when an attack apparently by Bosnian Government forces on two convoys under UNHCR and UNPROFOR auspices respectively led to 1 fatality and 10 wounded among the UN associated personnel, which resulted in the halting of convoys on that route for some time. Casualties among UNPROFOR

The Croat and Bosnian Government parties each complained to the UN of the other's continuing aggression and warned of the possibility of larger scale conflict unless these attacks were halted. The Bosnian Croats complained of Bosnian Government attacks against the Vitez enclave and asked for certain threatened Croat areas to be declared Safe Areas. The Bosnian Government complained of continuing Croat and Serb attacks, particularly by the latter both near Safe Areas and on Sarajevo itself. Subsequently the Bosnian Government's Prime Minister and the Prime Minister of Croatia met in mid-November to agree steps to reduce military hostilities in Bosnia and to enable the movement of humanitarian aid, also renouncing force as a means of resolving issues.

In his report of 7 January 1994 on the situation in Bosnia and Herzogovina, the UN Secretary-General stated that innumerable cease-fires had been agreed and signed by all parties but practically none had been honoured. Even the Christmas Truce worked out under European Union auspices in Brussels on 22 December had failed. The continuing level of violence in Central Bosnia was disrupting UN humanitarian aid, all the more vital as winter set in. In spite of higher level agreements by the warring parties to aid this traffic, only 50% of the required level was getting through. Not only were the convoys subject to attacks both indirect and direct, from all three sides, but bureaucratic procedures imposed by the parties further disrupted the flow of supplies.

The proposed reinforcement of UNPROFOR approved in June had still only seen fewer than 3,000 of the additional 7,600 troops arrive in the theatre and in some cases national contingents lacked the necessary equipment to carry out the roles required, meaning that help had to be sought urgently from other nations to equip them.

With regard to specific locations such as the Safe Areas, although the Bosnian Serbs had not yet withdrawn their heavy weapons out of effective range, the presence of UNPROFOR units had apparently deterred any further ground incursions although Sarajevo on 4 January 1994 alone received some 1,470 shells.

With regard to another key point, the airport at Tuzla, a major priority for the flow of humanitarian aid, the local Bosnian Serbs had still not agreed to its being opened for flights. However although UNPROFOR had declared itself willing to consider opening the airport without Serb agreement, the governments participating in the airlift to Sarajevo as well as others that might fly into Tuzla had made it clear that such flights required concrete guarantees from all sides: especially the Serbs.

Following UNPROFOR's mandate in Bosnia to help maintain the humanitarian aid lifeline through Sarajevo airport and then by convoy to other areas since June 1992, many thousands of humanitarian aid flights have landed at Sarajevo; by December 1993 the RAF alone had made over 1,000 flights carrying almost 14,000 tons of stores and many humanitarian convoys have been facilitated, the British battalion having escorted more than 70,000 tons of supplies in over 1,580 convoys.

Nevertheless the continued fighting in central and southern areas undermined the humanitarian effort. In spite of higher level agreements and even factional regional commanders' approval, UN Forces escorting humanitarian convoys have faced physical obstructions to their movement through the use of mines and road-blocks usually manned by small groups of combatants who sometimes refuse to accept orders from their own higher commanders. Indeed each separate road-block can demand a completely fresh start to the dialogue and appeal process up the factional chain of command. In addition the deliberate destruction of routes and instances of deliberate targeting of UN vehicles and personnel have further restricted the movement of UN elements. Another adverse factor, often ignored by outsiders, is the practical problem of vehicular movement in rugged terrain in poor weather, particularly in areas where route maintenance has suffered through neglect. Nevertheless, thanks to UNPROFOR's efforts, humanitarian aid is reaching the various destinations in Bosnia and Herzogovina on a regular basis.

However following UNPROFOR's mandate in Bosnia to help maintain the humanitarian aid lifeline through Sarajevo airport and then by convoy to other areas since June 1992, many thousands of humanitarian aid flights have landed at Sarajevo; by early October 1994 the RAF alone had made over 1,400 flights carrying some 19,500 tons of stores and many humanitarian convoys have been facilitated, the British battalion having escorted more than 150,000 tons of supplies in well over 2,000 convoys.

Of considerable importance are the developments in the early months of 1994 which have seen at least the first steps in a more hopeful scenario. On 6 February 1994 the new UNPROFOR commander in Bosnia & Herzogovina was able to negotiate a cease-fire in Sarajevo to take full effect from 25 February. The weapons' control measures he stipulated were supported by a NATO declaration on 10 February requiring compliance under penalty of air enforcement action. Under these measures heavy weapons, particularly those capable of indirect fire, were either to be placed in UN monitored areas or withdrawn an agreed distance: in the case of mortars 10 kms or more, while artillery (including tanks) were to be withdrawn 20 kms.

This requirement was complied with by the relevant factions with the result that the shelling of Sarajevo was brought to an end and activity could begin to restore damaged facilities within the city and to seek to develop normal conditions of life. Subsequent to the success at Sarajevo, the Bosnian and Croat forces also concluded a cease-fire on 23 February thus providing a further opportunity to rehabilitate areas and create conditions that will in the longer term reduce the need for humanitarian aid. Subsequent negotiations have resulted in a 'framework' agreement for a federal structure to embrace both Bosnian (Muslim) and Croat majority areas within Bosnia & Herzogovina.

The reduction of armed conflict through such measures were seen as essential because this would in turn free UNPROFOR resources from its duties in protecting humanitarian aid to turn to other tasks such as monitoring cease-fire agreements, the collection of heavy weapons etc. These new tasks pose additional burdens on the already stretched resources of UNPROFOR. In order to capitalise on the successes of February it has been necessary to redeploy some 1,200 UNPROFOR troops and 100 Military Observers from Croatia and elsewhere in Bosnia and Herzogovina into the Sarajevo area.

In March discussions were also underway as to whether the UN "Safe Areas" should be extended to include three further towns Mostar, Vitez and Maglaj. Initial assessments by UNPROFOR revealed that it already had a presence in the areas of Mostar and Vitez but to provide UNPROFOR support for Maglaj would require a considerable enhancement of UNPROFOR in the form of a heavy mechanised infantry battalion plus engineer & Logistic support - a total of some 1,500 additional troops. However provision by UN members including the UK who made a further infantry battalion available, enabled redeployment of UNPROFOR resources in late March to cover these new areas. These subsequent increases in UNPROFOR has brought its strength as at late September 1994 to 38,582.

Further UNPROFOR and the UN Secretary-General's Special Representative succeeded in March in obtaining general agreement to the use of Tuzla airport for UN Humanitarian aid flights. On 8 March a Nordic battalion took control of the airport and on 22 March the first UN flight landed there carrying both the UN Special Representative and the UNPROFOR Commander.

The Bosnian Government forces and Croation forces reached agreement in late February for a cease-fire in areas previously disputed which greatly reduced tension. In addition around Sarajevo with the UN presence backed by the UN enforced exclusion zone, the situation became more stable with transport routes into the city re-opened and a great reduction in the number of 'black market' operators.

However the area around Goradze became a flash-point in March 1994 as the small forces that the UN managed to move into the area came under attack in the course of a sustained Bosnian-Serb offensive. Eventually in the face of airstrikes against their ground positions by NATO aircraft called in support of the UN, a 3 km exclusion zone and a 20 km heavy weapon exclusion zone were agreed at the end of April.

Also at the end of April pressure from Bosnian government forces around the Posavina corridor led to heightened tension and risk of a major clash. Accordingly UN Military Observers deployed around Brcko thus providing a UN presence which helped reduce tension. In addition UN support for humanitarian aid convoys has seen routes operational into all parts of Bosnia with a much increased flow of supplies.

SUMMARY

In conjunction with UNPROFOR's action of the ground, the international community has sought to broker a generally accepted political settlement. The latest proposal - that of the Contact Group of USA, UK, Russia, France and Germany - has been accepted by both Bosnian Government and the Croatian party but to date the Bosnian-Serb group have still not agreed. Nevertheless in spite of this impasse and the frustrations that this engenders, UNPROFOR's presence has clearly stabilized the ground situation, reducing or ending fighting in many areas.

In considering UNPROFOR's performance, it must be remembered that its organisation reflects its mandate to operate through agreement rather than through enforcement and that this will inevitably influence the measures which it is able to take in seeking to fulfil the mandate.

It should be added that although the delivery of humanitarian aid has tended to be the most high profile of UNPROFOR's tasks, it should not be forgotten that UNPROFOR's presence in the Safe Areas of Bosnia and Herzogovina has had the beneficial effect of stabilizing the ground war in these areas and has prevented any direct ground incursions of these, or their loss to besieging forces, although indirect weapon attacks unfortunately do continue in several areas.

MACEDONIA

In November 1992 tension in the Kosovo province of Serbia between Serbs and the Albanian ethnic majority, led to concern about the safety of Macedonia which might be drawn into any conflict between Serbia and Albania and that fears Serbia had designs on dominating Macedonia, if not actually annexing it.

Accordingly, following a report on the situation in Macedonia to the UN Secretary-General by a UNPROFOR mission, he recommended in his report on December 1992 to the Security Council that a small UNPROFOR presence should be established on the border of the Former Yugoslav Republic of Macedonia (FYROM) to act as a deterrent and to monitor and report developments that could threaten the stability of FYROM. This was agreed in Resolution 795(92) of 11.12.92. The numbers agreed were: a small UN Force HQ, 35 MILOBs, a battalion of 700 UNPROFOR troops covering the western and northern areas, 23 UNCIVPOL to monitor the activities of the local police and a small UN civil affairs staff.

The UN force, initially from UNPROFOR's Bosnian contingent, arrived in early January 1993. In February a composite Nordic battalion arrived freeing the first unit to return to Bosnia. On 15 June the Secretary-General advised the Security Council that the United States had offered to contribute 300 troops to the UNPROFOR presence in Macedonia and this was accepted by Resolution 842 (1993) of 18 June 1993.

The small UN force in Macedonia, now just over 1,100 strong with a small number of Military Observers and UN Civilian Police, has continued its work of monitoring and patrolling and has been instrumental in reducing tension. The main problem now facing the area is largely economic as a result of the Greek economic blockade and the international sanctions at present in place against Serbia.

SUMMARY OF UNPROFOR IN FORMER YUGOSLAVIA

UNPROFOR's mandate has dictated its organisation, strength and deployment. As a peace-keeping force, it can only fulfil its Mandate with the co-operation of the different parties to the conflict. Unfortunately these parties expect UNPROFOR to carry out only those parts of its Mandate which would improve their own position. UNPROFOR's popularity is undermined as each side blames it for failure to fulfil their expectations. This has led to dissatisfaction with UNPROFOR, with propaganda and threats against the Force from all parties, escalating to harassment of UNPROFOR vehicles and men and in some instances direct attacks.

The experience of UNPROFOR on the ground is that, a peace-keeping force, mandated to work primarily through co-operation, this means that negotiation, arbitration and conciliation are the key features of successful operation, particularly within such volatile conditions. The UN forces reflect this is their conduct of their missions through a pragmatic, practical approach seeking success through co-operation which is likely to be longer-lived than that resulting from attempts at coercion. This pragmatic approach is rendered all the more important by the unclear demarcation of the warring factions at many points and their use of indirect fire weapons from covered terrain. Attacks can be launched by one party seemingly from the territory nominally under control of another making anything other than a clear sight direct fire response uncertain of hitting its proper target and thereby failing to achieve any benefit that might accrue to such action and risking making a difficult situation worse. However UNPROFOR has shown itself prepared to defend its personnel and its Mandate and has most recently reinforced this through the use of selected close air support strikes against forces attacking UNPROFOR units.

It is significant that in spite of the difficulties, both the Force Commander and the Secretary-General consider that UNPROFOR's presence has had a positive effect in containing a volatile situation and assisting in the furtherance of humanitarian and efforts by the UN and NON Governmental Organisations and with the help of UNPROFOR, there are signs of progress towards meaningful negotiations between the different factions.

The Secretary-General has recently pointed out UNPROFOR is not mandated, equipped, trained or deployed to be a combatant force. Rather it is a widely dispersed, lightly armed peace-keeping force and that a change in its role to a more combative one, inevitably putting it unambiguously on one side in the conflict, would have consequences unlikely to lead to a durable peace and would require the UN Force's withdrawal.

UNPROFOR : FACTS

Location:

a) Croatia, province of former Federal Socialist Republic of Yugoslavia.
b) Bosnia-Herzogovina, province of former Federal Socialist Republic of Yugoslavia.
c) Macedonia, province of former Federal Socialist Republic of Yugoslavia.

Duration:

12 months initial deployment. Extended from Feb 1993 for further 3 months and subsequently further extended.

Function:

a) Croatia.
Demilitarization of UN Protected Areas (UNPAs) containing ethnic minorities: protection of UNPA through deployment of UNPROFOR, UN military peacekeeping force and UN civil police. Thereby to create conditions of normality to allow negotiation of overall political settlement between majority and minority ethnic groups.

Mandate subsequently extended to include 'monitoring' of normalization of conditions and the re-establishment of Croatian administrative control of "Pink Zones" (Serb controlled area of Croatia outside UNPAs), but with protection of (Serb) minority groups within these Zones.

Further duties on immigration and customs functions with regard to international borders with UNPAs to check UN arms embar goes, and additional monitoring of demilitarization of certain areas and monitoring of 'no-flight' solutions of UN Security Council.

b) Bosnia-Herzegovina.
Protective support for Humanitarian Aid including control of Sarajevo airport as main airlift lifeline. Extended to include Military Observers to monitor humanitarian situation within UN recom mended 'safe areas'. Subsequently also monitoring of UN 'no flight' resolutions to prevent combat air sorties thus reducing the level of violence.

c) Macedonia.
Monitoring of any developments in border areas which could threaten stability of Macedonia.

Authorization:	Recorded in the following UN Security Council Resolutions:
Resolution No Date	**Resolution**
743 (1992) 21/2/92	Establishes UN Protection Force (UNPROFOR) in Yugoslavia for initial period of six months.
749 (1992) 7/4/92	Authorises full deployment of UNPROFOR; calls on parties concerned not to resort to violence.
758 (1992) 8/6/92	Enlarges mandate and strength of UNPROFOR.
761 (1992) 29/6/92	Authorises SG to deploy additional UNPROFOR units to ensure security of Sarajevo airport.
762 (1992) 30/6/92	Urges Croatian withdrawal, authorises strengthening of UNPROFOR, reaffirms arms embargo.
764 (1992) 13/7/92	Authorises further UNPROFOR deployment to protect Sarajevo airport and humanitarian deliveries.
769 (1992) 7/8/92	Authorises enlargement of UNPROFOR's mandate and strength.
776 (1992) 14/9/92	Authorises further increase in UNPROFOR strength and mandate as recommended by SG.
779 (1992) 6/10/92	Authorises UNPROFOR to monitor JNA withdrawal from Croatia and demilitarisation of Prevlaka Peninsula.
781 (1992)	Bans military flights in Bosnian 9/10/92 airspace; requests UNPROFOR to monitor compliance.
786 (1992) 10/11/92	Approves strengthening of UNPROFOR to include monitoring Bosnia no-fly zone.
795 (1992) 11/12/92	Authorises SG to establish UNPROFOR presence in Macedonia.
802 (1993) 25/1/93	Demands end to Croatian attacks in UNPAs and return of heavy weapons seized from UNPROFOR control.

Resolution No Date	Resolution
807 (1993) 19/2/93	Demands end to deployment of forces in UNPAs and pink zones in Croatia; extends UNPROFOR to 31 March 1993.
815 (1993) 30/3/93	Approves SG's report on UNPROFOR and extends its mandate to 30 June 1993.
816 (1993) 31/3/93	Bans all but humanitarian flights over Bosnia; states states able to enforce compliance after seven days.
819 (1993) 16/4/93	Demands that parties treat Srebrenica as a safe area; demands end to Bosnian-Serb attacks.
824 (1993) 6/5/93	Declares Sarajevo, Bihac, Gorazde, Zepa, and Tuzla safe areas.
836 (1993) 4/6/93	Enlarges UNPROFOR's mandate to include protection of safe areas.
842 (1993) 18/6/93	Welcomes contribution of troops to UNPROFOR in Macedonia.
844 (1993) 18/6/93	Reinforces UNPROFOR to protect safe areas in Bosnia.
847 (1993) 30/6/93	Extends UNPROFOR's mandate to 30 Sept 1993.
869 (1993) 30/9/93	Extends UNPROFOR to 1 October 1993.
870 (1993) 1/10/93	Extends UNPROFOR to 5 October 1993.
871 (1993) 4/10/93	Extends UNPROFOR to 31 March 1994 and calls for revival of Joint Commission to help restore the the Republic of Croatia's authority in UNPAs.
900 (1994) 4/3/94	Calls on all parties to co-operate with UNPROFOR in consolidating the cease-fire around Sarajevo.
908 (1994) 31/3/94	Increases force total by 3,500 troops to implement the cease-fire. Mandate extended until 30 September 1994.

914 (1994)

Increases force total by further 6,500 to implement the cease-fire between Bosnian government and Croat forces.

Strength:

As at 17/9/94 Total strength for all three areas: approx 38,582 of which 624 UNMILOB (frm 32 countries) 641 UNCIVPOL plus 1870 civ admin staff.

Contributors:
(troops approx numbers, some still deploying

Argentina (1,000), Belgium (730), Canada (2,000), Czech Republic (750), Denmark (1,300), Egypt (400), Finland (300), France (5,900), Jordan (3,000), Kenya (900), Luxembourg (90), Malaysia (1,500), Nepal (900), Netherlands (2,000), New Zealand (250), Norway (600), Pakistan (3,000), Poland (900), Portugal (10), Russian Federation (1,100), Slovak Republic (600), Spain (1,100), Sweden (1,200), Turkey (1,500), Ukraine (600), UK (3,300), United States of America (700).

Estimated Costs:

For period 12/1/94-31/7/94, assessed cost = US$2.1 billion. The monthly rate has now risen from $65 million to $140 million reflecting the increased strength and additional operational requirements.

Casualties:
(as at 15/3.94)

924 including 79 fatal.

Printed in the United Kingdom for HMSO
Dd. 298023 C100 1/95